Raising Capital for Real Estate: A 3-Hour Crash Course for Beginners

How to Create Passive Income from Home and Captivate Investors, Provide Credibility and Finance Projects

Edward Day

from various sources. Please consult a licensed professional before attempting any techniques outlined in this book.

By reading this document, the reader agrees that under no circumstances is the author responsible for any losses, direct or indirect, that are incurred as a result of the use of the information contained within this document, including, but not limited to, errors, omissions, or inaccuracies.

Table of Contents

Introduction

"Ninety percent of all millionaires become so through owning real estate." -by Andrew Carnegie

American real estate has been one of the best assets a person could ever own. Over the past 100 years, the real estate market has returned an amount in excess of what the stock market has (*Capital Raised for Real Estate Investment Pre-Covid-19 Hits Record High*, 2020). This is despite the fact that the real estate market had a complete meltdown in 2008 when it crashed to multi-decade lows.

This scared away many people from investing in real estate, but the fact remains that real estate investing is one of the most lucrative ways for new investors to increase their net worth by large amounts. This is because there is always going to be a demand for housing.

People will always need places to live and to shop etc. Both residential and commercial real estate opportunities abound in America, and until the Covd-19 lockdown took place, real estate financing was at an all-time high.

There are many ways in which deals get financed. Traditional methods involve going to a lender and hoping and praying that you qualify for a mortgage. This is the route that many investors attempt, and they find their applications rejected more often than not. The fact is that traditional lenders such as banks are extremely risk averse.

As a result, they end up lending money to people who don't really need it in the first place. Is it any wonder that these institutions then need to turn to fancy derivatives to boost their returns? Most banks don't understand how real estate works and, as a result, the real estate entrepreneur isn't best served by them.

This is where private financing enters the picture. While such investors are willing to absorb more risk, sourcing such opportunities might be difficult for the average person. After all, it isn't as if you can hang a sign in your window and expect people to come flocking to you with bags full of cash.

If you've spotted a great potential investment, but don't have the money to turn it into a reality, it can be frustrating for you to watch someone else take advantage of it. So how does one go about raising money for real estate? How should you present yourself to investors, and more importantly, what sorts of deals stand a good chance of attracting money to them?

If you're looking for the answers to these questions, you've come to the right place! In this book, you're going to learn how fundraising for real estate investment works. More importantly, you're going to learn what the market looks like right now, and which inefficiencies in it you can take advantage of.

Risk and Opportunity

Despite the manner in which I just described traditional lenders, there's no denying that securing a loan from these institutions is the best option for many people. After all, the interest rates are the lowest and you're dealing with a large institution that is going to make sure you receive your money.

This highlights an important aspect of real estate, fund sourcing. While there are many options for you to raise money, not all of them might be suited for you. Some will work better, thanks to the low levels of risk present in them, while some might be horribly unsuited for the investment opportunity because of the terms being unsuited.

The task for the real estate investor to master is to fully understand the ins and outs of these methods, and that begins with fully understanding the risks of each financing option. A hard money lender might be the most willing to give you money, but they aren't the best choice over the long term.

Think of the various funding options you have as being different tools. Depending on the scenario, you need to use different ones or even a combination of them. For example, many investors use so-called bridge loans to refinance properties, in order to attract the best interest rates.

Some even opt for interest-only loans in order to boost profits. The level of risk is high with such loans, but the profits on offer are large. Many beginner real estate investors tend to shy away from running the numbers on their deal, but in order to boost your returns you need to fully understand how financing works.

This is just one of my objectives with this book. The other major objectives include helping you figure out where you can find investors, how to structure deals, and what to do when asking for money. All of these points are addressed in their individual chapters and you're going to find them dealt with in the most comprehensive manner possible.

You might be tempted to think that approaching an investor and asking them to invest money with you is a lot like a job interview. Well, this is right and wrong. You are asking someone for their help in order to go somewhere, and in this, it is like an interview. However, since you're asking them for money, you're a businessperson and need to present yourself as being a credible entity to invest with.

Most beginners struggle with that second aspect. They think credibility comes with experience, and experience comes with investment. However, investment comes with money and if you have no money, how do you begin? In this book you're going to learn how to break that wheel and start attracting funding for your deals.

The only question is: Why should you listen to me?

Who am I?

My name is Edward Day and my official title reads full-time Forex trader. I've been fortunate enough to be able to invest in a wide variety of real estate deals over the years but it wasn't always the case. I started off by earning a degree in accounting and worked as a chartered accountant for a few years after graduating.

While the pay was steady it wasn't earth-shattering and, it left me wondering whether there was more to life than just this. I felt as if I wasn't achieving everything that I was supposed to be. Luckily, one of my clients happened to be a full-time Forex trader, and he invited me to a seminar. I was hooked onto trading from that moment.

I began pursuing my dream of trading successfully, and even enrolled in college to earn a degree in economics to better understand the markets. In 2008, I was finally able to quit my job and rely full-time on my Forex trading. I was also able to invest my money in property deals, and these days, I earn a steady 12% return every year on my investments in this area.

Preparation has been the key to my success, and in this book, I'm going to walk you through all of the steps I took to achieve these returns. This book represents all the knowledge I've gleaned over the years. I'm not a self-professed guru by any means. I'm just a regular guy who managed to figure out how things work, and then executed simple principles.

This is what I'm going to help you do as well. Real estate investment might seem like a far away dream for you, but in reality, it's a lot closer than you think. This book will help you get closer to your dreams and will help eliminate the biggest obstacle most people have: Money.

Earning returns in real estate requires you to have money. If you can manage to convince other people to invest in your deals, you're going to find that your returns will be double that of the average returns most investors earn in the market.

So without further ado, let's jump right in and take a look at the various ways in which real estate deals are financed.

Chapter 1:

Raising Real Estate Capital

- The Best Methods

There are many ways of raising the cash you need to finance real estate deals. This chapter is going to help you compare all of these methods, and get to know the pros and cons of each. As I mentioned in the introduction, every financing method has its own unique risks.

What is undeniable is that, in order to be successful as a real estate investor, you need cash. You can either use your own cash or you can use other people's money. If you have your own cash, you would presumably not need to read a book such as this one. The thing about using other people's money is that it is a double-edged sword.

On one hand, your own returns will be massive from the investment. The flip side is that if you happen to lose money, you're going to be in a very poor spot indeed. Think of it like this. If you buy something worth $100 with $1 of your own money and borrow the remaining $99, you stand to make a huge gain if the investment doubles in price. However, if it declines by even 1%, you stand to lose 100%.

Therefore, no matter the financing method, you need to do your homework and get to know the numbers of the deal inside and out. There's a lot more at stake than just someone's money. You could find yourself losing a lot more than what you put in, if the deal goes sour.

Having delivered that warning, let's look at the different ways of financing you can make use of. These are:

1. Conventional loans
2. FHA loans
3. Adjustable rate mortgages
4. Private lending

5. Hard money lenders
6. Institutional investors

There are other methods of investing in real estate that require either little money, or provide alternative entry paths to real estate. These are real estate crowdfunding, micro loans, retirement accounts and peer-to-peer lending. These alternative methods are not the focus of this book, and I won't be talking about them in any kind of detail.

Briefly, real estate crowdfunding allows you to invest in real estate projects that are funded by a registered real estate crowdfunding company. These companies buy the property (or finance the mortgage on it) and sell shares in the project to individual investors. They require very little upfront investment, as little as $500 in most cases, and are a great way to get started if capital is a huge issue for you.

Micro loans refer to small loans that financial institutions provide investors with. The application process for these loans is less strenuous than with a mortgage. However, the scrutiny levels will be close to the same if you fail to make payments. Usually, this is not a problem because the loan amounts will be small. If you have cash and need just a little bit more to finance a property, this might be a good choice for you.

If you've saved up enough in a retirement account, or if someone in your family had bequeathed the cash to you, you can use this cash to invest in real estate. There isn't any special method of coming up with the money here, it's just a situation that some people are lucky enough to have in their lives.

Lastly, you can apply for a loan from a peer-to-peer lending platform. The loans sourced from these platforms are usually provided to pay off credit card debt, but there isn't any restriction on the use you can put the money raised to. As long as you're transparent about how you'll be using the money, you stand the chance of being funded by a crowd of people.

This is crowdfunding as well, but in a slightly different manner. The flip side of this method is you won't be able to raise too much money. After all, no one is going to fund a $100,000 debt so that you can go ahead and use it in real estate. Smaller loan amounts are entirely possible, and like micro loans, you can use this if you're facing a shortfall.

Now that those alternatives are out of the way, let's take a detailed look at the first realistic option you have: Conventional loans.

Conventional Loans

These are the most common type of financing used by investors, and are also the easiest to understand. The other term used for such loans is mortgages. The terms of a mortgage are pretty simple. You apply for a loan, the bank lends you the sum of money at a certain interest rate, and you need to pay it back within a certain time period. Throughout this repayment period, you'll be paying a monthly sum that includes both interest and principal payment.

Principal refers to the amount of money you've borrowed. Banks will usually lend money to real estate investors at a loan to value (LTV) ratio of 80%. This means you'll need to come up with the cash needed to finance at least 20% of the deal.

If the property is worth $100,000, you'll need to pay $20,000 as a down payment, in order to secure the deal. The mortgage application process is one of the most dreaded events in any person's life, but it's far simpler than it's made out to be. The reason most people dread it is because they aren't adequately prepared to handle the demands of the lender.

The Process

Preparation is the key to having a smooth application process. The first step in this regard is to first figure out how much cash you can afford to pay down. If you have a property in mind, understand that you'll need to finance at least 20% of it yourself. Now, you might not have the cash lying around so you'll need to come up with a plan to save this amount of money.

The next item to take a look at is your Fair Isaac Corporation (FICO) score. This is colloquially termed your credit score, and is an important part of your application. Typically, banks and traditional lenders want to see a credit score north of 700. Anything below this makes approval hard.

Before you apply, you should seek to improve your score as much as possible. You can do this by reducing the amount of debt balance you carry on your borrowing channels, such as credit cards and on your car loan. Reducing credit card debt goes a long way towards increasing your score.

The other thing you want to ensure is that you have steady employment. Banks like to see stability in their borrowers, and for this reason, if you appear to be someone who switches jobs often, you're going to have a hard time qualifying for a loan. Generally, you want to remain at a single workplace for at least a year or two before applying for a mortgage.

In addition to this, you should not switch jobs when your application is under processing. This is a surefire way to get denied, no matter how solid your application is. Prior to applying, make sure you have enough cash saved up for the down payment, and that you've also set aside a sum to allocate for closing costs.

This is something many people neglect at first. Closing costs accounts for the fees of all the professionals involved in helping you push your deal through. The loan officer, the escrow agent, the real estate agent, the title company and the insurance companies are paid from this amount. Usually, the fees for closing range from three to six percent of the total property value (*Real Estate Project Finance - Know Different Funding Types*, 2020).

Collect all of your salary and income proofs before applying, as well as proof of income-tax filings and so on. You'll also need a letter from your employer stating that you're gainfully employed. If you're self-employed, it's going to be tough to qualify for a loan unless you've been running your business successfully for at least six years or so.

Once you have all of these in place, you should apply for what is called pre-approval. Pre-approval is a great way to receive a ballpark figure of how much a bank will be willing to lend to you. This way, you can look at properties that are in your range and not waste time on deals that are outside your budget.

Financial Worthiness

The bank's aim during the pre-approval and approval process is to calculate how likely you are to make your monthly mortgage payments. To do this, they calculate two ratios. The first is called the front ratio. This is calculated by dividing your projected monthly mortgage payment by your monthly salary before taxes.

Banks look for a value under 28%. If you earn $3,000 per month, and if your mortgage payment is under $840, your lender will be happy with this. The second ratio is called the back ratio, and is calculated by dividing the sum of all your debt payments (including the projected mortgage payment) by your income.

The lender looks for a value of under 36% for this figure. Given your $3,000 per month income, your total debt payments need to add up to under $1,080 per month. These ratios are rules of thumb and in real life, lenders might be willing to stretch them given special circumstances.

If you have a high degree of cash savings, or if you happen to have an inheritance of some sort, then the bank might be willing to lend you the money even if you're above these threshold limits. Coming in under these limits is no guarantee of being approved. Every lender has their own idiosyncrasies, and you might find your application being rejected for one reason or another.

Rejection is not the end of the road. You can always reapply or provide additional documentary evidence that shores up your case. Mortgages are mostly used to finance residential real estate property. In the case of commercial property it takes a lot to be financed.

This is because commercial property is viewed as being risky, and the banks require a lot of documentary evidence of business success before financing such deals. First time commercial real estate investors typically don't bother approaching banks because there's no way they'll ever qualify, unless they happen to be introduced through someone else.

Why would someone subject themselves to such a lengthy process such as this? Simply because of the many advantages that this mode of financing offers.

Advantages

The biggest advantage of traditional financing is that mortgages are readily available and are provided by almost every bank out there. One of the first things you'll be hit with when you open a new bank account is the offer of a home loan at attractive interest rates.

There's also a large support network for mortgages, in the form of real estate agents and other professionals, that is used to dealing with these forms of financing. As a result, you're not going to lack any professional support throughout the process, and you'll find them ready to assist you with the finer points of your application.

The terms and conditions of a residential real estate mortgage are also straightforward. The interest rate is fixed, your monthly payment is fixed, and you can easily calculate how much you have left on your loan. You can even prepay your principal amount ahead of time to reduce your amount owed without incurring any fees.

Commercial mortgages usually cannot be prepaid unless you're willing to pay a penalty. This is because banks earn money off the interest, and they will demand compensation in case you pay your principal early.

Lastly, traditional lenders offer the best mortgage interest rates, and this will save you close to five figures on a property when compared to the interest rates offered by alternative lenders. Most people don't mind the lengthy process and the mountains of paperwork they need to file. Just remember to be prepared ahead of time, and use the pre-approval process to waste as little time as possible.

Despite these advantages, there are many downsides to the traditional mortgage process.

Disadvantages

The two biggest obstacles to securing a traditional mortgage, are the down payment amount and the requirement that you need to have a good credit score. Banks are extremely traditional and set in their ways when it comes to lending to individuals and small entities. They don't mind gambling their money with Wall Street, but if an individual changes their job midway through the application process, they're deemed too risky to lend to.

While credit scores can be improved, they take time to do so. If you've amassed too much debt on your credit cards, or have gone through bankruptcy in the past, you can wave your chances of qualifying goodbye. The best thing to do is to seek alternative sources, or use the next option I'll be highlighting.

Another drawback is that you cannot have multiple mortgages. This limits your chances of expanding your investment portfolio, and you'll need to carefully choose the deals you're looking to participate in. It also means you'll need to exit out of one deal before participating in another.

A technique that rich investors like to use is to invest in property through a limited liability company or LLC. This is a good way to limit any liability that you might incur on the property. However, this method is not accessible for first time investors. You can form an LLC, but the bank will not lend you the money unless you have a good relationship with them, or if the LLC has a significantly profitable track record.

In short, banks try to lend money to precisely those people who don't need it. It can be frustrating dealing with them, since they tend to function like large machines. The loan officer reviewing your application doesn't have much power in the process and is simply following a set of rules they have to stick to.

Despite all of this, if you manage to qualify for a loan, then you'll find that they're a great way to increase your net worth. The fact that you can negotiate almost every point in the loan agreement is another advantage. Secure a low-interest rate, and you'll manage to grow your wealth even faster than projected.

Federal Housing Authority Loans

Also called FHA loans, these are provided by the FHA. The FHA is an organization that was set up by the government to ensure that Americans always had a go-to resource when it came to financing home purchases. The FHA loan application process is very similar to that of a conventional mortgage application.

However, the requirements for qualification are a lot lower. The way it works is that you approach an FHA lender and apply for a loan. The FHA approved lender can be a traditional lender as well. With conventional loans, the mortgage is kept on the bank's books. Therefore, the bank absorbs all the risk inherent in the mortgage. However, in the case of FHA loans, the bank transfers the mortgage to the Federal government. The government can absorb a fair number of hits and defaults, and therefore, it can afford to relax lending standards considerably.

With this in mind, the credit score requirements, as well as the LTV ratios on FHA loans, are much better for investors that don't qualify for conventional loans. While conventional loans require applicants to possess credit scores above 700 (roughly), FHA loans reduce this requirement to 580.

While traditional lenders require you to place 20% down on purchase, the FHA requires you to place either 3% or 10% down, depending on your credit score. If your score happens to be above 640, you'll only have to pay 3% down. These terms mean that a far larger number of people qualify for home loans with the FHA than they do with conventional lenders.

The only caveat with the FHA loan scheme is that the property must be owner-occupied. For this reason, many real estate investors don't use this scheme. After all, you cannot use an FHA loan to rehab a property, and then resell it into the marketplace.

The FHA is vehement about not allowing home flippers to profit from it. In fact, properties that are being resold, within three months of being bought by someone else, are not eligible for FHA financing. For example, if a home flipper (someone who buys run down homes and rehabs them) buys a property in January, and tries to sell it in April, and if you're trying to buy this property with an FHA loan, you can't do so.

In some cases, this limit is extended at the discretion of the lender. All of this means, there's just one investment strategy that applies to FHA loans, and that's house hacking. This is when you purchase a multi-unit property, and then live in one of the units yourself. Some people house hack single-family properties by renting out individual rooms as well.

Despite the limited scope of investment strategies available, FHA loans are a great deal for those that can qualify for them. Because your cash invested in the deal is as potentially low as 3%, you can recoup it extremely quickly.

The FHA also runs another scheme called the 203(k) loan, which can be used for home improvement. The credit score requirements for these loans are a bit higher. You need to be 640 and above to qualify. You can however use these loans to rehab a property. The catch is you need to occupy it yourself.

Therefore, you can combine a house hacking and rehabbing strategy to realize a huge amount of wealth from these loans. The appraisal process is the most crucial part of the entire loan application process. This is when an FHA approved home appraiser will take a look at the property, and will evaluate whether it is eligible to be financed.

They'll also affix a value to the property, and this determines the loan amount. If the property is far too rundown and needs extensive work, the FHA will not finance it. In all other regards, the application process is exactly the same as with conventional loans.

When it comes to payments, FHA loans are a bit different from their conventional cousins (Merrill, 2020). There is a thing called private mortgage insurance or PMI that you need to be aware of. PMI is insurance that the FHA seeks in case you default on your payment. This is a monthly payment that is attached to your mortgage payment.

With conventional loans, you need to pay PMI only if your down payment is less than 20%. With FHA loans, you pay it for the entire term of the loan. Make sure you check what this payment figure will be. Despite the higher down payment requirements, the lack of PMI on conventional loans means that you might end up paying less for the duration of the loan.

Let's look at the advantages of going down the FHA route now.

Advantages

The ease of qualification is the biggest advantage of an FHA loan. Given the low credit score requirements, a larger number of people qualify for them. They also place a smaller financial burden on borrowers, since the down payment is a lot less than usual. The closing costs remain the same, but the lesser down payment means you don't need to spend years saving up for it.

There are a large number of lenders that participate in the FHA's program, and as a result, you won't find it a problem to apply for this loan. Like with conventional loans, there is an army of professional support to help you throughout the process, and you don't need to worry about being left to handle everything by yourself when applying.

Disadvantages

The requirement regarding owner occupancy is the biggest drawback of the FHA process. What's more, you need to occupy the place for at least a year. Since you cannot apply for another mortgage during this time, you're stuck with your property for at least this amount of time before you can cash your investment in, and move onto another property.

While this is a good thing for first time investors, it's frustrating for those who have already been around the block a few times. It does delay the rate at which you can grow your investment.

The viability of the FHA loan process hinges quite a lot on how the appraisal is conducted. Home appraisers are well-trained in every aspect of their job and are required to be licensed in order to carry out inspections. The industry is well regulated, but every now and then disagreements can crop up.

If the appraiser marks a property down for too low a value, and if the seller doesn't reduce their price, then you'll have a shortfall to cover. The appraiser will also inspect the property thoroughly, and this involves its own headaches.

Lastly, there is no way the FHA will ever fund a commercial property. You're stuck with residential real estate. This isn't necessarily a bad asset class to be stuck in, however, it does limit your options in case you find a good deal on a commercial property.

Adjustable Rate Mortgages

Adjustable rate mortgages, or ARMs, made news for all the wrong reasons back in 2008. Back then, they were being used to finance homes that borrowers had no business purchasing. They were being used by unscrupulous lenders to generate as many loans as possible on their books so that they could be offloaded to Wall Street banks, who then repackaged them and sold them to investors.

ARMs are a speculative tool and if you happen to qualify for one, you can bet that the bank issuing the mortgage to you is not carrying the risk on its books.

Here's how they work. The mortgage has a fixed term like a conventional mortgage, and has the usual 20% down payment requirement (for the most part).

What it doesn't have is a fixed interest rate. Instead, it has a rate that fluctuates with the prevailing market conditions. If the interest rate environment is low right now, you'll have access to a low or teaser rate. When interest rates go higher, your loan's rate will increase along with it.

The interest rate doesn't have to be tied with the larger real estate market or interest rate index. It could be tied to some other obscure index as well. Some ARMs aren't even tied to an index and function like credit card interest rates. You might have seen some of these offers.

Pay zero percent interest for 12 months, and then pay a fixed rate forever. Using this for credit card debt is one thing, but when it comes to a mortgage, the ramifications are very real. Most people in 2008 went from making payments of $150 per month to $1,000 on their home loans.

This is because the teaser rates, which were unconnected to reality let alone an index, were used to rope them in. Once the real rates kicked in these, people ended up being foreclosed on. The ARM world is diverse and there's no limit to how your interest rate might fluctuate.

For example, you could have a truly speculative ARM where the interest rate goes down as well as up. Typically, you won't find banks lending you money this way if you happen to be a novice investor. Such investors receive ARMs that contain rising interest rates. The banks figure they can get away with issuing such terrible debt to applicants.

Down payment terms also vary with ARMs, and every loan is its own individual deal. What I mean is that the lender will typically be a lot more open to negotiation with such mortgages than normal. After all, they stand to make more money and are risking a lot less on such deals. They can offer more generous terms if it's advantageous to them.

You will find some ARMs have a zero down payment option while some might require a higher than 20% down payment as a result. There is no fixed template to how this works. With adjustments possible over the entire life of the loan, there is no limit to how much the banks will be willing to negotiate terms.

A cousin of the ARM is the interest-only loan. This is a far more practical option for the real estate investor. Interest-only loans involve payments that are fully interest-based and don't have a principal component to them. Traditional mortgage payments have both contained within them, as you've learned.

Opting for an interest-only loan might make sense if you've run the numbers on your deal thoroughly. Banks are willing to extend these terms to the investor because they make money on the interest and not on the principal repayment. Investors for their part get to pay a lot less than normal because the principal isn't being repaid.

So how does this help them? Let's say an investor puts $50,000 down on a property (20% of total value) worth $250,000. They earn rental income worth $2,500 per month from this property. Let's say costs account for half of this amount, so their net income is $1,250 per month.

Assuming a 4% interest rate on the mortgage, their monthly payment will work out to around $830 per month. This means they're getting paid $420 per month to own the property. This comes to $5,040 per year. If the bank lends them interest-only terms for four years, they'll earn a total return of $20,160 over the course of these four years.

That's a 40% cash-on-cash return. Usually, investors use this money to make improvements to the property in order to increase its resale value. If the improvements bump property prices up to $300,000, then they've earned a 100% return on their cash investment. At this point, they'll sell the property and remove their cash out of it.

As you can see, this method is not without risks, and this is why only experienced investors should opt to implement this. You'll need to be aware of how the local real estate market works, and have a good amount of experience to demonstrate to the bank that you know what you're doing.

You should also understand that qualifying for interest-only mortgages is a lot harder than qualifying for regular mortgages. Banks will want to see a higher amount of cash invested in your bank account.

This brings us nicely to the advantages and disadvantages of ARMs and interest-only loans.

Advantages

Much like how you can use interest only mortgages to achieve a quick cash-on-cash return during that period, you can use the initial teaser rate period on the ARM to earn a huge profit. You will need to line up a lot of things, of course, but this is manageable if you know what you're doing and have executed your investment plan properly.

The speculative element of an ARM means that, if the interest rate index your loan is tied to remains low, you'll end up paying a low-interest rate for the duration of the loan. This can be a huge boost to your wealth and equity in the property when compared to a traditional loan.

The same advantages are inherent in an interest-only loan as well. Both loan types provide the savvy investor with the means of increasing their net worth dramatically.

Disadvantages

While the speculative elements of ARMs can be an advantage, more often than not they turn out to be a disadvantage. A truly speculative loan is unlikely to be extended to a regular investor, and as a result, you'll find that most ARMs issued to you will be of the teaser rate variety.

This means an increase in interest rates definitely will occur, and you'll end up paying a large amount of money when the real rate kicks in. If you find yourself being offered a zero down ARM then be very wary. While the terms of this loan might seem attractive, the fact is that you'll end up paying an arm and a leg when the real rate kicks in.

Given the low LTV of such loans, the monthly payment will be astronomical. Most beginners are best served by staying away from these loans. Seek conventional or FHA financing before trying to apply for these loans. You'll do yourself a favor by waiting for a bit longer before trying to boost your returns through these loans.

Private Funding

Leaving the world of banks and traditional lenders, we now enter the domain of mom-and-pop funding. This method of funding involves asking your family members and those close to you for help in funding your deals, and it can be a great way to get started with real estate investment, if you've done your homework correctly.

This mode of investment is actually used by a large number of beginner investors. Most people struggle to come up with the money for their down payment and closing costs, because of the high cost. Not everyone has the foresight or the life situation to be able to plan for a home purchase in advance.

As a result, they turn to family members in an attempt to fund their down payment. While they eventually return the money or treat it as a gift, some investors choose to use this method to provide their lenders with equity or a share of the profits from the deal. This is especially useful when it comes to pooling funds together as a family, or as a syndicate, in order to finance a lucrative investment.

Some people even choose to run an entire portfolio in this manner, with one person being the designated investment manager. It has the potential to build wealth for everyone involved to a high degree. If you're familiar with the way real estate investment trusts work, then this is a private version of that business model.

The way it works is that you pool funds together, and then sell shares in the private fund to your individual investors. The fund earns an income from the rents and the capital gains that arise from the property price appreciation. There are a lot of advantages to this method of raising money.

Advantages

The biggest advantage is that you can set terms as you wish, as long as your investors are on board with you. You'll be dealing with people who are close to you, and you'll be able to gain their trust a whole lot easier. These people will have known you for a long time and, as a result, you don't have to worry too much about trying to impress them with fancy figures.

You might also find it a whole lot easier to explain your investment thesis to them. Typically, when making real estate investments, people stick to their local area, since so much of real estate success depends on the local market cycle. Therefore, your investors will also be familiar with the local area, and you won't have much trouble convincing them to come on board.

Aside from the need to not necessarily have pitching experience, or even investment experience, you can offer them a lot of flexibility in terms of how you wish to raise funds. You can opt to give them a share of the profits, or you can offer them a fixed payment or a debt structure in exchange for their money.

The choice is entirely up to you and the person investing, and everything is up for negotiation. You can launch your partnership in this manner and seek out properties to invest in.

Disadvantages

Despite the advantages of this method there are a few disadvantages you need to be aware of. First off, you'll be doing business with those that are close to you. While this can be an advantage, it can also create situations where you won't be able to make a rational decision. If anything goes wrong, it's not just money you could potentially lose, but the relationship as well.

The fallout from things going wrong is what deters most people from asking their friends and relatives for money. Besides, not everyone has friends and relatives who are rich or can afford to stump up enough cash to finance real estate investments.

You'll need the services of a good lawyer to create agreements that leave zero room for error or misunderstanding between you and your partners. This is simply being careful in most cases, but when it comes to those close to you, it's doubly important to avoid any potential misunderstandings down the road. So make sure you invest in one if you do choose this option.

Lastly, while this is a great way to get started, it's hardly an option for long-term growth, unless you happen to have a billionaire relative. At some point, you're going to have to seek other forms of funding to fuel the growth of your investments. However, it is a great way to get started on that first property.

It does raise the stakes of the investment though, and some people don't like this sort of pressure. If the investment goes wrong then you might not be able to raise money from these people again, and might lose credibility with them in your personal life as well.

Hard Money Lending

Hard money lending can be both a boon and a curse, depending on how the investor uses it. For starters borrowers who happen to have bad credit, and have no familial means of raising money, will have to resort to this type of borrowing. Hard money lenders can be far more flexible in terms of approval, but the risk is higher for the borrower.

For starters, you're not borrowing from an institution, but form a smaller network of investors or even an individual. These lenders aren't too concerned with your credit score, but will take the value of the property into consideration. The property will serve as collateral for the loan.

This means if you default, you'll lose the property and any benefits you gain from it. Something that increases the risk of these loans is you'll need to have built at least 30-40% equity in the property. Hard money lenders finance projects at 60-70% LTV, at the most.

Thus, if you're completely skint, you can't use this option, unless the property happens to be a gem in the making. Sometimes, the lender will base their loan amount on the After Repair Value or ARV. This increases the risk for the lender and thus, you won't find them offering this option to newbie investors.

The interest rates that are offered on hard money loans are also on the higher side. In most cases, these are around 10-15%, which is pretty high. These interest rates don't change too much based on the national economic picture. Instead, they fluctuate depending on the level of competition a lender faces.

For instance, California has uniformly lower interest rates because of the large number of lenders operating in that state (*Hard Money 101: Everything You Need To Know About Getting Started With Hard Money Loans*, 2015). Every hard money lender has certain types of properties they specialize in.

Generally speaking, hard money lenders will not cross these lines since they place a great value on their ability to value a deal. Residential property lenders will not finance commercial properties and vice versa. In some situations they might be willing to do this, but this only happens if there's another lender present who's willing to pool funds and has the expertise in the property.

Typically, you'll make interest-only payments over the year, and at the end of the term you'll need to make a balloon payment (which is a higher than usual amount hence the term.)

Let's take a look at the advantages of opting for a hard money lender.

Advantages

The lack of a high credit score or even concern about your credit history is the biggest advantage with a hard money lender. They're only concerned with the value of your property, and don't really care if your record has a foreclosure on it or a bankruptcy. If you have these on your credit record, then using a hard money loan can be a great way to bounce back and rebuild your wealth.

The terms that are offered are also flexible. Usually, the terms are offered for a year. The implicit understanding is that the borrower will build equity in the property over a year's time, and will then refinance the property and enable the lender to earn the 10-15% profit that is the interest on the loan.

For this reason, hard money payments don't include any principal repayment and are interest only. This reduces your cash outflow burden considerably, and you'll be able to boost your returns in the property.

If you're flipping properties or are seeking funds to develop property, then hard money loans are your best bet. Most borrowers use these as a bridge loan. When starting out, the borrower doesn't qualify for traditional financing. However, after a year, once equity is built up and the project has some financial backing behind it, banks are more likely to finance it.

Thus, the loan bridges the gap between where the investor started out and brings them to a state where they are creditworthy for banks to lend money to. The loan approval process for a hard money loan is pretty straightforward and involves an examination of the property itself.

Every point of the deal is negotiable. This means you don't have to rely on the opinion of a single appraiser, and have the means to question any appraisal estimate the lender uses.

Disadvantages

While hard money loans have a lot of positives for the new investor, they can pose some risks for them as well. For starters, the money is expensive. 15% interest rates are nothing to sneeze at. Most of this payment is made at the end of the term through the balloon payment, which is where you'll have to return the principal as well if you cannot secure refinancing.

This is the biggest risk with bridge loans, and it is something your lender will also take into consideration. How likely is your property to be refinanced? If the chances of refinancing are remote and if the project contains too many risks, then your interest rates will increase even further.

At the end of the year, if you haven't secured enough financing, you'll need to either sign up for another year's worth of expensive payments or you'll need to find some other alternative. Worse, if the property cannot sustain your interest payments, then you'll end up losing it since the lender will seize it as collateral.

The application process can also be less structured, and you won't have any professional help that will explain the finer points of the deal to you. This doesn't mean you'll be swindled. Hard money lending is fully regulated in the United States. However, you could end up with a loan with terms you don't fully understand.

So make sure you understand the terms and conditions fully, and don't be afraid to ask questions. Some investors choose to remain silent for fear of appearing less than credible. However, it's better to look clueless once, than to have it come back and bite you down the road.

Another disadvantage is that you need to have enough equity in the property. This means you'll need cash. In most cases, you'll need even more cash to invest in the property than what a traditional lender would require. This defeats the purpose of approaching a hard money lender for most investors.

After all, the reason they approached them in the first place was because they were having problems financing their property purchase. If this situation applies to you, then you'll have to seek alternatives or simply save enough cash to invest in a deal down the road.

Investors

If none of these options are viable for you, then seeking investment from a private investor or a fund might work. Typically, funds require the borrower to have significant experience investing in real estate. For the first-time borrower, approaching an angel investor might be their best bet.

Angel investors typically assume far higher levels of risk than banks or even hard money lenders do. They're willing to invest in long shots in exchange for a large payoff. This means your deal needs to be a potential home-run in the making, and not a run-of-the-mill kind of a deal.

If you manage to source such a deal, then an angel investor will be more than willing to provide you with all the funding you need. The manner in which you approach an angel investor is extremely important. Remember they don't know you, and as a result, the way you present yourself often makes or breaks the deal.

I'll cover how to approach potential investors in a later chapter. For now, just keep in mind that it isn't your experience, but your confidence in the deal, that matters the most. The way you convey the opportunity and describe the advantages of the deal in terms they understand is extremely important.

Angel investors will usually not fund debt, but will instead seek equity in your deal. The investors who operate in the space also have experience dealing with such projects, and you'll find them more than willing to share their experiences with you and even mentor you as you execute the project.

Keep in mind that despite their risk appetite, you'll still need to invest your money into the deal. No investor is going to stump 100% of the cash required and settle for 50% of the profits. You might find that you'll have to settle for a finder's fee or even sweat equity, which amounts to around 15% in such deals.

The toughest part of getting financing through this method is finding an investor. I'll cover this in detail later in the book. For now, let's look at the advantages and disadvantages of seeking angel funding or institutional funding.

Advantages

If you're starting out with real estate investing, then you'll find that the expertise an angel investor brings to the table will be invaluable. You'll be able to use their experience and contacts to ensure your project turns into a success. Another advantage that angel investors bring to the table is their patience.

They're used to taking risks with regard to investing, and generally possess tons of patience as long as you're executing the deal properly. This is in contrast to a bank or hard money lender who is concerned about getting paid every month no matter what the deal looks like. As such, angel investing can reduce the pressure you feel in terms of delivering results.

Given that, these investors take an inequity stake in the deal, they're taking as many risks as you are, if not more. Your cash flow burden is reduced or eliminated completely and is a factor only when profits are generated from the deal. In many cases, if it's prudent to reinvest these profits back into the property to generate even more cash, an angel investor will be on board with this.

With regard to institutions, these advantages play out on a much larger scale. You will find these companies more willing to give you some leeway in terms of cash flow produced, but given the presence of investors on their own books, institutions might not have the same levels of patience as a single angel investor might.

Having said that, they're still far easier to deal with than banks. As long as the deal is being executed properly, you'll find them on your side, and you'll be able to leverage their experience and network, much like with an angel investor.

The mere presence of an institution on board with you is often a great sign of success by itself. After all, these companies don't back duds, and if you manage to convince them to join you, obviously something is right about the opportunity you have on your hands. The same can be said for the presence of an angel investor as well, albeit on a smaller scale.

If the deal goes well, you'll find them willing to invest even more funds into the project. They're businesspeople at the end of the day and aren't a bank that's solely concerned about the amount of interest it earns. As a result, you'll be able to realize the true potential of the property by aligning yourself with these kinds of investors.

Disadvantages

There are some things to keep in mind when approaching an angel investor or an institution. While angel investors might be willing to work with beginner real estate partners, an institution most definitely won't. In fact, it might be hard for you to even get your foot in the door with such companies.

You'll need to have a solid track record and the network to back it up. Without this, institutional investment might be inaccessible to you. Angel investors will be willing to work with you, but be prepared for a laundry list of questions about the project and about your own experience.

Many investors find this process tough and a bit distasteful. If you're well-prepared and if the deal really is a good one, then you should have no issues with this. This doesn't alter the fact that you're giving them a share in your deal. In most cases, the angel investor ends up taking a greater equity stake in the deal.

This happens because they're the ones putting up all the money. You might get either a finder's fee if they're willing to execute the deal themselves, or you might end up with sweat equity if you're the one putting in the work.

Many beginner real estate investors are naive about the way equity splits work and expect a 50% stake in the deal just because they 'found' it. It doesn't work that way. Sweat equity amounts to 15% at the most, or 20% if you're lucky. A finder's fee is typically between 5 to 10%, depending on the deal and how well you can secure it.

This might lead some people to become disappointed. If you can manage to secure debt financing from one of the previous options, then this might be a better choice for you in the long run. Essentially, you'll be a glorified manager in such deals. This isn't a bad thing, but if you're harboring hopes of being a major player with your first deal, you'll need to realign your expectations.

The investor or institution will have a say in how things are run. After all, they bring immense experience to the table, and they will want to have a say in things. You might need to swallow your pride and do what they say. This might not be a bad thing in terms of deal execution, but if there is a personality clash or a difference of opinion, you're not going to win that argument anytime soon.

Despite these disadvantages, there's a lot to be said in favor of going down this route. Just make sure you're willing to put up with the negatives of this mode of investment, in order to realize the positives.

This brings to a close a look at the various ways in which real estate deals can be funded. As you can see, there are different methods of sourcing funds, each with their own pros and cons. Make sure you understand what goes into the various funding methods and how they affect your deal's cash flow, and what your relationship with the funding party will be.

Chapter 2:

Preparing to Impress

Potential Investors

Knowing the various sources of funding is one thing, but securing them is entirely another. How you present yourself to investors in order to gain their trust is crucial. Investors are seasoned professionals and have been around the block a few times. They know what a good deal looks like. There are two points on which you might be rejected.

The first is that the deal might just not be good enough. The second is that you might not be credible enough to partner with. In the case of conventional financing, credibility simply extends to your financial means and your existing debt levels. In the case of angel investing, your professional portfolio and the way you present yourself is also a part of the equation.

This chapter is going to give you the lowdown on how to prepare to present your deal to investors. Keep in mind that not all of the steps outlined here might be necessary for every single financing option. For example, if you're looking for a conventional mortgage, then preparing a pitch deck is unnecessary.

The theme throughout all of the points in this chapter is that you need to convey authority and credibility. You need to present yourself as someone who knows what they're talking about and has the drive to execute your plan. Keep this in mind as you read the material.

Before preparing to pitch your idea to potential investors, you will need to prepare. What does preparation entail exactly?

Task One: Prepare

This task contains three subtasks. Your goal should be to:

1. Understand the market
2. Familiarize yourself with the potential investor's needs
3. Educate yourself with regard to terminology to build credibility

Understand the Market

This is the biggest task ahead of you. How does one go about understanding the market? The good news is that, when it comes to real estate, you don't need to focus on broad economic factors very much. Instead, simply taking a look at the local market and property value trends is more than enough. This is because real estate values depend on local factors far more than they do on national ones.

The best place to begin is online. Websites such as BiggerPockets and other real estate oriented forums will help you understand how the real estate cycle works. The best part is that you'll be able to network with other investors in your area. Many areas have real estate investment clubs that host regular meetings.

Make it a point to attend these meetings and network with the people there. You don't have to be on the lookout for investors all the time. Networking with fellow newbies will help you immensely, since you'll be able to relate to what they're telling you a whole lot better.

The advantage of building a local network is that you'll be able to receive different perspectives on the market. For example, a developer will look at property differently than a flipper or a contractor. Contractors and appraisers are invaluable resources to have because they'll usually give you the real deal on what a property is worth.

Remember that when it comes to conventional financing, an appraiser's words are what count the most. The bank is going to listen to them at the end of the day. Getting to know them and how they think about property will help you understand the difference between a selling price that is a pipe dream, and the real value of the property.

There's no standard template as to how all of this works. Simply look to develop relationships with people and you'll find that you'll end up educating yourself in real estate lingo and market cycles. Aside from networking, online market research is also extremely helpful.

For instance, websites such as Zillow, Loopnet and Roofstock, are extremely useful when it comes to figuring out property values in your target area. Zillow even contains prior sales listings that you can look at to develop a rough comparative value of the property in question. If you haven't sourced a deal as yet, these websites will help you locate them.

Good old-fashioned driving for dollars also works wonders; drive around the neighborhood in question and look at the different kinds of properties that are present there. Looking at pictures online is one thing, but you'll get a real feel for the neighborhood when you physically move through it.

You might be thinking of rehabbing a property development into an apartment complex for young professionals. However, if the neighborhood doesn't offer the quality of life such people will be after, your plan is dead in the water. Always assume that your investors are experts in the properties in an area.

This means they know the history and property values of pretty much every deal in the area. Adopting this mindset will drive you to learn everything you can about property values in your area of interest. Examining the demographics and quality of life factors goes a long way towards understanding the area.

After all, the primary motivation behind investing in a property is to be able to place it for rent, or to resell it for a higher value after rehabbing it. In order to do this, you need to understand the kind of buyer that will be on the lookout for these properties. Examining the quality of life offered, is the best way of understanding what these people will be looking for.

What is the crime rate like? What are the quality of schools nearby? Who are the biggest employers in the area? What is the type of property on offer in the neighborhood? Often you'll find that an area will be divided between prosperous and less than prosperous based on an arbitrary division in the neighborhood. Perhaps south of a particular street property values drop precipitously, despite belonging to the same locality.

Get to know all the quirks of the neighborhood in question, and do your research. Network with other investors and real estate professionals in the area, and you'll soon get to know how things work locally.

Your Potential Investor's Needs

As wonderful as you are as a person, your investors aren't giving you money because of this. They're in it to make money. How well do you know and understand your potential investors' needs? What kind of a return are they expecting, and how well are you poised to give them this?

Further complicating this question is that different investors have different needs. Banks are concerned with earning interest every month while angel investors are looking for massive increases in equity. You'll need to tailor your pitch accordingly to their needs.

What's also important is for you to figure out what your own needs are. If you're giving up equity in the deal, you're reducing your potential earnings from the property. This reduces your cash outflow, but it also limits the rewards. Are you willing to work on the deal for this? In some scenarios, opting for conventional financing might be the better bet.

Most real estate investors get so lost in their need to find financing, that they neglect their own needs. The result is they end up striking a deal with someone that is unsuited to their own needs, and find themselves working on deals they have no enthusiasm for. You might have to absorb higher levels of risk in order to extract the value you're looking for.

For example, opting for an interest-only loan with the intention of extracting as much value from the property before selling it for a profit is a risky move. However, if you think that any reward that is less than what this method gives you is not worth it, then you'll be best off working this way.

When it comes to institutional and angel investors, understanding their portfolio needs is also important. Like hard money lenders, these parties specialize in certain types of property. If your angel investor is looking for a different type of property for their portfolio, then bringing this sort of a deal to their attention will go a long way towards convincing them to join you.

For example, if a well-known property angel investor has a full portfolio of residential deals already, no amount of convincing on your part is going to get them to sign up to your deal. You'll need to take into account what they're looking for, as well. Institutions are extremely risk averse in terms of building a portfolio.

They have specific thresholds and concentrations that they adhere to at all times. They do not exceed allocations towards property types or deal sizes. They have investors to answer to, and as a result, you won't find them breaking their rules even if your deal is a sure shot (Han, 2020).

Take these factors into account by asking them what sort of deals they're looking for. This will help you avoid wasting your time trying to convince them when they aren't in the market to begin with. These entities will have large networks, and by letting them know what you have to offer, they'll be able to put you in touch with someone who might be interested or better suited for your purposes.

Of course, you'll still need to come across as being credible, but targeting the right people based on their needs is a good first step to take. It saves everyone a lot of time, and then you'll be able to get your deal in front of the right people.

Educate Yourself

This ties in with establishing credibility. You might have found a great deal and might understand the financials of the deal in your own language, but unless you speak the investor's language you're not going to go anywhere. You'll need to educate yourself on the jargon and terminology that is applicable to the space.

Real estate is notorious for having a ton of rules of thumb and abbreviations that scares away many beginners. Terms such as REOs, NOI, cap rates, ARV, ROI, the 50% rule, the 70% rule, 1031 exchanges, and so on, might make it seem as if real estate deals are complicated.

However, once you begin to get into the details of what these things are, it really is quite simple. What's more, real estate offers you a lot of flexibility in terms of structuring the deal. If a deal is too complex, then you're under no obligation to enter into it. Many investors think that complexity is a sign of genius, when it really signals incompetence.

If you meet someone who loves throwing jargon around needlessly, you're talking to an amateur. Don't come across as someone who does this. Experienced investors can spot these people a mile away. Instead, be upfront about your experience (or lack of it) and demonstrate that you have educated yourself in the various aspects of real estate investment.

This mostly applies to equity investors. When it comes to traditional lenders and others who offer debt financing, letting them know that you have the ability to execute the terms of the deal is important. They're more concerned with the value of the property itself than in your own credentials.

To this end, do your homework with regard to what they're looking for. For example, hard money lenders usually require a low LTV value. If you haven't invested any equity in the property or aren't in a position to do so, then don't waste your time and theirs by approaching them for a loan.

You might even have to combine a few funding sources to strike a deal. You could raise money from family and friends for a down payment, and use that as an equity stake to convince a hard money lender to come on board. How well do you know the property and the metrics this person will be looking at?

Do you understand what the ARV and how it will be affected based on the repairs you carry out? Have you spoken to a contractor and received a rough estimate of repair costs? Showing the lender that you've done your homework and are up to speed with regard to all of their requirements, is a great way to build credibility and make it easier for them to give you money.

Central to all of this is your investment pitch.

Building an Impressive Pitch

Every potential investor, be they debt or equity based, will need to be pitched. How well you tailor your pitch to the investor's needs, and how well you can understand what to mention in your pitch, is critical for your success. This section is going to walk you through the best methods of putting together a great pitch that will help you succeed more often than not.

A pitch isn't always needed. In the case of a conventional loan application, you're not going to have to put together a pitch deck. Your application itself is your pitch, and this is a rigid form that doesn't give you any leeway to improvise. In such cases, it's best to do your homework and work to reduce your debt levels.

In short, present a picture that the lender wants to see. They want to see low risk in lending to you. This means you'll be able to prioritize your mortgage payment and will be able to make payments on time, every time. Have a decent amount of living expenses as cash balances in your bank account, over and above your down payment expenses.

This will let them know that you'll be in a good position even if you happen to lose your job or source of employment. Do not carry student loan debt under any circumstances. This will bury your application in the undesirable pile as soon as the loan officer sees it. Besides, it isn't prudent to borrow money for a mortgage just to clear student loan debt.

Having an established pattern of expenses is also a good idea. Don't overspend too much on a month-to-month basis. The idea is to give the loan officer a good idea of how much you spend monthly, on average. Too many spikes in spending might flash risk to them. All of this might seem like overkill, but it's how the system is set up (Han, 2020).

Once you have the mortgage in hand, do whatever you want to do, within reason. If you want to qualify for a conventional mortgage, you'll have to play by the lender's rules. A good way of making the system work for you is to apply for an FHA loan, if it suits you, instead of a traditional bank loan. The down payment requirements are far lower, and your cash investment is less as a result.

For all other financing needs, you'll need to prepare a pitch deck of some kind. A hard money lender isn't going to want to see a fancy PowerPoint presentation from you. However, you'll need to put together something to let them know what the deal is all about. The more effectively you understand and tailor your message to their needs, the better.

Niche

Every investor will be looking at different numbers. However, no matter what the investor's focus is, it all comes down to numbers. A hard money lender is concerned with the ARV of the property. I've already described what this is. As a result, they'll be scrutinizing the degree of repairs needed and the cost of those repairs.

Before approaching such a lender take the time to inspect the property and make detailed notes about what is needed. Keep in mind that, in a lot of cases, cosmetic repairs dramatically increase the value of the property. A lick of paint and better door handles can easily bring in an additional $200 per month in rent.

The critical areas, from a tenant's standpoint, are the kitchen and the bathroom. Install good-looking, but cheap, fixtures in there, and you'll drive the value of rents upwards. From the lender's perspective, focusing on these aspects and displaying your knowledge of the costs of these cosmetic repairs, will convince them that you know what you're doing.

If you happen to have a property that requires a deep level of rehabilitation, they'll focus on your experience. As a beginner to real estate, it's probably best that you stay away from such deals. Build some experience first before jumping into these. In fact, this is what most investors will also tell you.

My point is that your pitch will need to focus on different metrics depending on who it is being shown to. Make sure it focuses on the numbers that the investor will be interested in. The hard money lender is not going to be too interested in the demographics and the renter's profile. All they're concerned about is your ability to pay them interest over the course of the year. Showing them renter profiles and detailing your plans to entice them, doesn't really add anything for them. It does however, make a huge difference to an angel investor or to your friends and family.

These people are investing to take a cut of your profits, so you'll need to detail where these profits will come from. While you don't need to change your pitch to suit every single person you present your deal to, you do need to niche it based on the type of deal you're pitching to them, and on the kind of investment they're offering you.

No matter who the investor, is it comes down to two numbers: risk and returns. Risk is a vast area and includes qualitative and quantitative metrics. Some investors will solely evaluate risk in quantitative terms. For example, a conventional lender looks at your front and back ratios to determine the risk of payment default.

Angel investors will take qualitative factors into account. Do you seem to know what you're doing, and do you present yourself as a serious person? These things matter a lot to private investors, but not so much to debt investors, whether private or FHA. In terms of returns, there are different metrics the investors might look at.

A private investor who is investing in equity will be concerned with the cash flow possibilities of the property. The hard money lender, on the other hand, will be far more interested in minimizing costs and maximizing the amount of property appreciation that can be realized. This is despite the fact that the hard money lender will not be getting any share of the capital gains from the price appreciation. They'll still be concerned with the ARV because that represents your gain, and you'll be paying them from that amount. So despite this being a metric that doesn't directly affect them, they'll use it to scrutinize how good of a deal this is.

Talking to your local and online network will help you tailor your pitch a whole lot better. As much as possible, speak to lenders and other investors in different areas to understand how you can tailor your pitch to appeal to people like them.

Showing this sort of interest will enhance your credibility and will brand you as someone who's honest and willing to work hard to make sure deals go through.

Structure

The way you structure your pitch is extremely important. This is irrespective of whether you're presenting your pitch verbally, or if you're presenting it formally to a group of people via PowerPoint or some other tool. Investors are concerned with getting down to the important points of the pitch, which are the numbers and what's in it for them.

However, it still pays for you to spend some time crafting intrigue about the opportunity. You don't need to get cheesy with this or deliberately delay getting to the point. However, you should tell them a good story before you get into the details. Everyone loves a good story and investors are no exception.

This is especially true if you're pitching an angel investor or an institution. By story, I'm not telling you to get carried away and write something that Hemingway would be proud of. Instead, give your deal a relatable model. For example, if you're pitching a rehab project, highlight the relevant numbers in a snapshot.

Do you expect to earn a 50% return on the deal? Framing it as a project that earns these levels of returns, with minimal risk, is a good way to create a story around it. Think of your story as being a quick introduction to what your pitch is all about. Remember that your investors are coming into this meeting cold, and know nothing about the opportunity.

Show them why they need to spend time looking at your deal. Most beginners will jump right into the complexities of the deal, however, most investors are not ready to do so right off the bat. They still haven't received a reason from you as to why they need to take you seriously. Give them this reason by focusing on a quick summary of what the deal is, and tie it to a theme that they can relate to.

Once this is done, feel free to focus on the details. There is a balancing act you'll need to carry out here. You want to give them details, but avoid going into so much detail that it buries them with questions and confusion. A good way to get this balance right is to give them 90% of all the information you have about a topic related to the deal, and let them ask you questions about the remaining 10%.

This is a good way to get them involved in the pitch. By asking questions, they're investing effort into analyzing the deal, and by answering their questions, you're establishing yourself as an authority in the subject. These two things combined, greatly increase your odds of being funded.

Let them know what the target market is like and the relevant demographics. The detail with which you dive into this depends on the type of investor you're talking to. This applies to every relevant point about your deal and investment opportunity.

Perhaps the most important point about your deal is to highlight the revenue generation model. In other words, how will you make money? Explain how this works and give them all the details they're looking for. Make sure you present the information in a way that is easy to understand.

Most real estate investors will be good with numbers so don't be afraid to use them if you're pitching someone verbally. Carry documents that back your projections as much as possible, but focus on giving them the real numbers. You can even be conservative with your estimates and your investors will appreciate this.

A common mistake is to overdo the marketing aspect of the deal and promise ridiculous returns to the investor. You'll only come across as someone who isn't worth spending time on, and will attract investors who are themselves not serious about their business. Be professional and conservative in your estimates and you'll attract people who are worth working with and spending time with.

Pitch Decks

A pitch deck is a formal presentation that highlights the important points of your investment opportunity. Truth be told, you won't need to prepare these unless you're presenting to institutions. Some angel investors might insist on these if they happen to believe in a formal process.

Pitch decks usually combine revenue and profit projections, with costs and investment needs. In short, they detail the financial roadmap of the project. They also cover every relevant aspect of your deal.

Structuring a pitch deck might seem like an intimidating task, but there's a simple way to do this. The first two slides of your pitch should be an elevator pitch. This is where you'll provide your investors with a quick summary of why you're presenting to them and what your deal offers.

Think of this as a hook that gives them a reason to keep on reading or listening to you. These two slides will also help you organize your own elevator pitch in case you meet someone who can be a potential investor, but hasn't come across your deal as yet. It'll help you condense the most relevant points of your deal, and get the benefits across to your potential investor quickly.

Once this is done, you'll need to go into the details of your deal. This should be simple to do if you've done your homework. What are the demographics of the area, why is this deal attractive for an investor, and what sort of returns they can expect? Make sure you create a financial roadmap as well.

What will your expenditures be in the first few months or phases of the project? When will your investors begin to see some of their money being returned to them? Do you foresee any reinvestment needs?

Most importantly, what is your exit strategy and contingency plan in case this fails to materialize? Will you hold on to the property and refinance it? Or will you look to sell it to another investor for a profit?

Use your pitch as an opportunity to evaluate the strength of your deal and your ability to execute it. A detailed pitch deck will help you identify any weaknesses and will give you the opportunity to address these weak points.

Qualitative Aspects

While the numbers are an important part of your deal, your pitch shouldn't be solely focused on them. You'll need to address the other parts of your deal as well, such as your marketing plan, your exit strategy and any sales strategy as applicable. It's easy to get caught up with the numbers and neglect these points, but this is where you'll be making the money in the deal.

Most beginners to real estate investment underestimate the amount of marketing it takes to see a deal through successfully. Consider a simple rental investment. You'll need to really think about how you'll market your property in order to attract the right type of tenants.

Good quality tenants will ensure you have steady cash-flow from your property and that you won't have to worry about too many headaches from them. The way you market your property is critical. First off, you'll have to make sure the neighborhood supports the kind of lifestyle they demand. Next, you'll need to have support structures in place that deal with any issues right away.

If a door knob falls off, or if some light fixture needs replacement, a high-quality tenant will want these issues addressed immediately. The more you delay, the less likely it is that they'll renew their lease. You'll need to also think about how you can earn more rental income from the property in order to make more money.

Perhaps making your building pet-friendly might result in higher rents? The flip side is that you'll have to pay special attention to how well the property is maintained. If you make the property accessible by wheelchair for the differently abled, this involves costs, but you can charge higher rents.

All of this ties your marketing and revenue generation plans together. You'll need to focus on both aspects in order to convince investors with regard to the finer points of your deal. This is just an example of how the process works when considering a rental property investment.

If you're developing property, then you'll need to have a sales strategy in place that attracts high-quality buyers. You'll need to return your investors' money in a timely fashion, so the efficacy of your sales tactics is important. Your pitch deck needs to dive deeply into your sales strategy and the related costs you'll incur.

Don't have a single line item in there that says 'Facebook ads' or something of this sort and leave it at that. This is the easiest way to lose all credibility you've built thus far in the process. You might need to hire people to market your property to realtors, and pay listing fees on major websites.

Account for all of these costs and leave yourself a buffer in the budget to account for unexpected expenses. What will you do if the prices of property fall while you're developing it? Do you have a contingency plan in place for this? What kind of returns will your investors have to look at if this happens?

Outline the worst-case scenario and let your investors know how their money will be returned to them. The point is to present a thoughtful and well-rounded picture to them, so that you build credibility as well as let them know of all aspects of the deal. Again, don't be tempted to present an overly rosy picture, or paint the deal as being a can't-be-missed opportunity.

These kinds of tactics work on low-quality investors. Experienced real estate investors understand how to value the positives and negatives in a deal, so don't worry about coming across as being less than 100% positive. Your aim is to be honest about the terms of the deal. You'll attract high-quality investors who'll help you with the deal as well as stand by your side when things get tough.

Be Prepared

Be prepared to answer some of the most common questions that angel investors will ask you. Specifically (*Top Questions Angel Investors Will Ask Entrepreneurs*, 2016):

1. What is unique about your deal? In response to this question you can highlight the financial opportunity that is in place, or some facet of the deal that is being overlooked by the market.
2. How big is the opportunity? This is a simple question to answer. Simply hit them with your elevator pitch that highlights all of the benefits of the deal.
3. What is your experience level? If you have enough experience this should be easy to answer. If you don't, be upfront about it and

explain why you're still suited to lead the deal and why it'll be a success with you at the helm. Explain the work you've done and highlight relevant examples of why you'll succeed at this.

4. How does the deal work? This is when you can get into the details of the project and run them through all of the relevant numbers.

5. Why has no one else spotted this opportunity? Are you missing something? There's no standard template in response to this question. You'll need to explain why you've managed to locate this deal, and why others have not been able to jump in on it. Highlight one of the entry barriers to this deal. Whatever you do, don't say "I don't know".

6. What are the marketing costs you'll incur? What is the cost of acquiring a customer? You'll need to project these and compare it to the profit you stand to earn when you make a sale.

7. What does the sales cycle look like?

8. What are your contingency plans? In case things go wrong, what does your worst-case scenario look like? Make sure you detail the worst-case scenarios properly and communicate to your investors what happens to their money. Keep the focus on how they'll make their money back and in what amounts at all times.

9. What are the legal or regulatory risks? This usually applies to commercial properties. Make sure you're up to speed with all regulations surrounding the property.
10. What are the financials and how have you arrived at these projections?
11. How much money are you looking for? This one is self-explanatory, and hopefully, you won't have any problems explaining this.

Build Credibility

The manner in which you conduct yourself throughout the process will go a long way towards building credibility in the eyes of your investors. Having said that, you'll need to leverage a few other channels to be able to appear as someone credible in their eyes. These days, this is relatively simple to do, thanks to the power of social media.

First, create a LinkedIn profile, if you don't have one already. In your profile, make it clear that you are active in the real estate space and are looking to put deals together. Publishing relevant content on your profile is a good way to get noticed. Join real estate investment groups on there and network with other people in them.

Having a profile on popular forums, and answering and asking questions on them also helps boost credibility. Remember, your investors are going to conduct a thorough background check on you. They are going to ask everyone they know about you, and appearing to be someone who is active in the space is to your benefit.

You can even start a YouTube channel and post a few videos where you talk about your deals and provide advice on whatever you know of. You don't need to be an influencer or some celebrity. Simply publishing content on YouTube goes a long way towards building credibility.

Another option is to start a blog. It doesn't have to be a fancy one, even a free blog will do. Link all of your social media channels together, and keep publishing relevant content. You don't need to write 2,000 word treatises on how real estate works in your area. However, showing that you're active and are keeping tabs on the market, is a great way to show investors you're serious about your deals.

If you have the expertise, host a webinar or create a course that teaches people how to invest in real estate, or take them on a journey with you as you source deals, and walk them through the finer points of it.

Maintain a professional web presence and you'll have no problems presenting a professional and credible profile to your investors. All of this goes a long way towards increasing your chances of getting funded.

Chapter 3:

Finding Investors

Now that you know what to say, the task facing you is to go out and actually find these people. This is problematic for a lot of beginner investors. Where exactly do real estate investors hand out? Do they have a secret society you can infiltrate? The reality is far more mundane than this.

Finding investors for your project is more an art than a science. You never know when you might run into someone who can fund you. All you can do is try through the usual channels and hope to find someone who can fund you. This doesn't mean you need to hinge your hopes on a wish and a prayer.

There are a ton of steps and strategies you can take to locate these people. You'll need to consistently expend effort on finding them. It is tough going at first. You'll probably run into a few people who have no business having any money, and yet appear to be extremely knowledgeable.

It'll be frustrating dealing with such people, and you'll be liable to think all investors are a bunch of jokers like these people. However, once you get past this lot, you'll find that serious investors do exist. While you do need to focus on finding investors, it pays to think of the process as screening and attracting the right kinds of people to you.

If you present yourself as a serious and realistic professional, you're going to screen people that have the same qualities. You'll attract investors that are looking to work with serious people and are willing to take risks in order to back sound deals. If you present and shop your deals around as can't miss opportunities, and as possessing unlimited return potential, you're going to attract unrealistic investors who will bail the minute things get tough.

So keep this in mind as you read this chapter. As important as it is for you to expend effort finding investors, you need to be someone who is worthy of their attention. This doesn't mean you have to have tons of experience. As long as you're upfront and honest about what it is you possess, and what kinds of deals you're looking at, you'll attract the right investor to you.

Networking

The oldest method of finding real estate investors still works like a charm and is the best way for you to go about finding the right investor. There are many different activities that come under this subheading. For starters, you should seek to actively participate in local real estate investment clubs.

You'll find listings for these clubs in popular event platforms, such as Meetup or some other network. If you live in a neighborhood that has a community center or some other location where residents gather, look for signs advertising such clubs. Alternatively, you could reach out to someone you know who happens to be active in real estate, and ask them for advice on how you can go about increasing your network.

These days, a lot of networking happens online. Forums and social media are the best tools to utilize. When it comes to forums, there are many small websites and communities out there that will help you educate yourself and will allow you to reach out to others in the space.

The social media site Reddit, is a great example of how different people can come together to create communities around virtually anything. Real estate investment is a huge topic, and there are tons of Subreddits (this is what communities are called on Reddit) dedicated to the subject.

Not only will you find communities dedicated towards fundraising, but also towards different strategies and localities. There is no limit really to how deep Reddit can run. The best part is that the people on Reddit are usually very sensitive to marketing, and as a result, you'll almost always receive correct information.

If you have any doubts about the investment process, or if you've heard some rumor or piece of information that doesn't quite ring true, then this is the best resource for you to use in order to check these claims. While you won't be able to always meet people on Reddit in real life, it is a great educational resource nonetheless.

I've already mentioned Biggerpockets, and this is a great website where you can learn a ton of information about the various types of real estate investment and also network with other website users in the forums. The forums on the website are pretty active and contain a lot of discussion about real estate topics.

One of the better features of these forums is that every user has a credential, so you can quickly figure out what their experience level is and how qualified they are to be providing that advice. While the advice might not always be foolproof, it will give you a good sense of belonging to a community that you can lean on.

On such forums, it's easy to find someone else who has already been through the process, and they'll usually be open to providing you with tips with regard to approaching a deal. Make sure to add some value back into the forum by helping others out, and you'll find these places to be a great source of information.

While institutional investors won't be hanging around there, you can bet that there will be people with money to invest who will be. What's more, a lot of experienced real estate investors often look to move into becoming the bank and expanding their property portfolio by investing in other real estate deals. Network with and build relationships with these people, and you'll find that fundraising won't be anywhere near as tough as it seems.

The key for you to remember is that these are real people. So don't be in a rush to try to cash in your chips. Always give value and you'll face no resistance.

Aside from forums, the other major online networking tool is social media. In this regard, there is only one platform you need to focus on.

LinkedIn

LinkedIn is often called the Facebook for professionals. However, the reality is that it is a far better engine and network platform than Facebook. While most people use the latter to promote their own special courses and mentoring programs, LinkedIn is where you'll end up meeting true professionals who actually know what they're talking about.

That self-help guru who's selling overpriced courses through his YouTube channel isn't going to be on the network. This is because the platform itself rewards high levels of credibility. People constantly use LinkedIn to find and network for business purposes. If you can afford it, paying for LinkedIn's premium features are worth every penny.

This allows you to connect and message people who aren't in your network. Statistics show that people respond to LinkedIn messages at a far higher rate than cold emails (Florentine & Kapko, 2019). If you're serious about finding investors then this might be a great investment for you.

Of course, it isn't as if people are on the platform with the term 'real estate investor' tagged to their profile. The ones that do are usually loudmouths who don't do anything. There are exceptions, of course, but you generally want to steer clear of such people. Instead, look to connect with real estate professionals in your area.

Look up your local realtors and agents and connect with them. Examine their networks and find other professionals such as contractors, title agents and so on. Title agents can be a great source of information since they'll usually know who is involved in the transactions that have been taking place. They won't tell you outright, but it can be helpful to get to know them.

Aside from fundraising, you still want to get to know such people because they will be your team on the ground. If you want to source great deals and arrange financing as quickly as possible, you'll want to have a framework in place that allows you to send and receive offers as quickly as possible. Networking with them is always a good idea.

You might even run into these people at the local real estate investment club. Make it a point to connect with them online as well. Keep posting relevant content with regard to real estate in your area and engage with the content they publish. In this manner, you'll always be at the forefront of their mind and will be able to leverage their skills should the need arise.

Your own profile needs to look professional and needs to communicate that you're in real estate in a serious manner. You don't have to be a professional (although this helps) working in real estate. As long as you can communicate that you are someone who is passionate about investment in this space, and are looking to connect with other enthusiasts and professionals, you'll be just fine.

Make sure you link to your YouTube channels or blog if you happen to be publishing them. Your goals shouldn't be to drive traffic but to establish the right kind of persona that a serious investor will want to see. They will check you out on social media and if they see that you're constantly in touch with other professionals in the field, are engaging with them and are publishing relevant content, this builds credibility.

Every once in a while you will find a wealthy real estate investor in the contact lists of the people in your network. When you find such people, connect with them and seek to engage with them first. A common mistake is to immediately ask them for money. This is a bit odd. Imagine walking up to a person for the first time and immediately asking them for some cash.

In real life no one would try this. The same rules apply online as well. Keep engaging them and after a while, reach out to them to check whether they're looking for new investments. If their profile mentions they're looking to invest, then you can message them immediately.

There are other social media channels such as Twitter or Facebook etc. Don't waste your time on these. Once you've built enough of a following, then you can use these platforms to spread the word about your campaign. However, if you're starting out, there's no chance of anyone finding you unless you spend an insane amount of time on these platforms.

For starters, Facebook's organic reach is limited to a maximum of 10-20 people or groups you engage with the most. The people outside this list will never see anything that you post. On Twitter, the same rules apply. Think of how long the average tweet remains in someone's feed after it's been posted. In the case of a busy social media account, it has a lifespan of around a second or two before a new tweet takes its place.

So don't waste your time on these platforms. Instead, look at expanding your reach organically on LinkedIn and through your blog posts. YouTube is also great for organic reach, so make sure you use this platform while this state of things lasts.

Unconventional Ideas

There are a few more ideas you can try to boost your networking in the real world. The aim with all of these is to get your name out there and let people know you're on the lookout for investors. The first and most obvious option is to let people around you and those in your investment club know you're looking at deals and are searching for investors.

Local community colleges and schools might have real estate courses that they offer. Reach out to them and offer to teach a class on the subject. You'll spread knowledge and you'll also develop a separate network of people who might be wealthy, but not necessarily active in real estate.

Join the board of local nonprofits and volunteer in their events. These events attract wealthy local people and you can get to know them better. This will lead to potential investment opportunities down the road for your business.

If you have the cash, then sponsoring some local event might also work. This typically is what developers do when they're looking to sell their properties. In addition to this, they also make use of local radio spots to spread awareness. This isn't strictly to do with fundraising but if your project involves selling the property in large numbers, then advertising in this manner beforehand helps a lot.

Another gold mine for you is to attend local conferences and industry events aimed at the real estate sector. While the association of mortgage brokers might not sound like a very attractive event, it pays to visit the place for a day at the very least. Every real estate investor can use a good mortgage broker. What's more, the broker will be able to help you smooth out any approval issues you've been having and will have tons of information on the state of the industry from the financing perspective.

Similarly, a conference aimed at the carpet installers association of America (I made that up, apologies if you happen to belong to it) sounds dull as ditch water, but it helps to meet these contractors and to understand what their rates are and how their business works. You might be able to reduce costs on your deal to make it even more attractive to investors.

The best way to approach networking is to do a little bit every day. If you look at the laundry list of items you can do, you'll likely be overwhelmed with information. Instead, seek to carry out one task every day and you'll soon build enough momentum to sustain your efforts. After all, you never know where an investor might materialize from.

Remember that all it takes is one good investor. Spread your net as wide as possible when searching for them.

Angel Investment Networks

Technically speaking, most angel investment communities tend to focus on technology and startup investment. When looking for angels, it helps to look for someone who has a real estate background or is interested in the subject of real estate. You should also take care to use your time wisely on these platforms.

This is because the time you spend on such websites and forums can be better spent on LinkedIn or real estate focused websites. However, it's best to cast your net far and wide since you never know who might be interested.

Keep in mind that some of these communities charge you a fee for access. Make sure the money is worth it before joining. This can be done by looking at the sort of people who join the forum in the first place. For example, any community that is connected to crowdfunding platforms such as StartEngine aren't worth it.

This is because that platform is used by companies to raise money through equity crowdfunding. As such, there is no real estate connection there for you to leverage. Thus, it would be a waste of time for you to spend time there. AngelList is an example of a forum that is frequented by angel investors from a wide variety of fields.

While the focus is heavily tech oriented, it might still be worth your while to explore the website and its communities. While these are not examples of forums, LinkedIn groups are great when it comes to networking. The problem is that there are just so many of them.

It might take some work, but it helps to try to start your own group on the platform once you've built enough rapport with other people in your network. Doing this will help position yourself as an authority, and you can employ rigid quality control on the types of posts that are published in the group. This in turn ensures high-quality people will join your group.

There isn't much more to say about angel investment networks. Search for them and make sure their purpose aligns with your objectives. Each network and forum has its own aims so make sure you're spending time on the right ones.

Pitch Nights and Investment Events

These events tend to be organized close to major metropolitan areas and usually occur once or twice every year. Some of them, such as Money2020 and WebSummit, are major events. While they aren't entirely focused on real estate, attending these events does help since you'll be able to get in touch with people who are looking to invest.

At the very least, you'll be able to network with other entrepreneurs who will be able to put you in touch with angel investors and other wealthy individuals who could potentially fund your project. I must mention that this is stretching your net pretty wide since most people attending such events will probably not be looking for real estate investment opportunities.

However, view this as a part of your regular networking efforts. In addition to this you'll also have the chance to view people pitching their product or company to investors, and can take a few tips in terms of crafting your own pitch and refining your pitch deck.

Accelerators

This is a fast-growing trend that not many real estate investors have taken advantage of as yet. The way accelerators work is pretty simply. They're traditionally focused on tech startups and upon admittance to an accelerator, they're provided with office space and resources to help them achieve exponential growth.

In the tech scene, growth is what's most important since this is what investors look for. Growth in that field refers to user-base and usage-time on the app or platform. In real estate, these metrics don't really apply and growth isn't always valued. However, there are other things that accelerators look for.

The viability of the idea and the entrepreneur's ability to scale their project, is something that is paid close attention to. A lot of accelerators are targeted at fledgling property development firms or other startups that aim to marry technology and real estate investment (Grozdanic, 2017).

As a result, you'll find that a wide variety of companies tend to get approved for initial funding. Admittance into an accelerator isn't a guarantee that you'll receive funds. However, it does make meeting angel investors and even institutions very easy. After all, you're in an environment where people are looking to connect with one another and place capital in deals.

Here are some of the most popular accelerators operating right now.

Fifth Wall

Fifth Wall is a venture capital firm that invests in the real estate and architecture space. As such, they've funded a wide variety of projects, from commercial real estate to real estate investment platforms. The fund runs an accelerator that is backed by a large number of construction firms and real estate companies.

Admittance to the accelerator is difficult, and your deal will go through intense scrutiny. Being a venture firm, they are looking for deals that are of a certain size and hold the promise of huge growth. Even if the fund doesn't directly invest in your deal, they facilitate meeting with the other sponsors of the accelerator and you might end up finding a large investor to work with.

The key is to think big with these deals. You can't approach them with a deal on a single family residence. Think more like 50 to 100 unit deals. After all, that is the size of the capital they have in hand, and in order to produce a return, they need deals of that scale.

AREA

This is an accelerator that is focused on tech startups in the real estate space. However, there's no reason why a traditional real estate project might not work if you align it to the goals of the company. For example, AREA is a major investor in Founder House, which is a co-living and co-working space for New York City area innovators.

There are many angles you can pursue by tailoring a traditional real estate investment to a tech oriented community building approach. It's a good way to gain equity or convertible debt funding for your startup. If you happen to diverge from the original path that you have thought of, you'll still have access to a property that can be refinanced and thus repurposed.

MetaPROP NYC

This is a New York City-based accelerator that provides funding upfront. They fund projects from across the real estate spectrum. Given that they're an accelerator, there is a tech focus inherent to the program. As such, raising money for a physical real estate deal that doesn't have any community building aspect to it is impossible.

However, if your project happens to have such a crossover, then this is a good option to choose. Every project is provided with $250,000 to start with and is given free office space in New York for 22 weeks. At the end of this period, the company might decide to fund your platform further, or they might connect you with other investors who might be interested in your project.

These sources of investment are a bit out of left field. They aren't completely focused on traditional real estate investment models. For example, rocking up to them with a deal for a 100 unit property might not appeal to them. Given that they're so tech focused, you might need to think laterally to have your project appeal to them.

If old-fashioned networking fails you, then utilizing one of these avenues might work for you. Keep in mind that you'll need to demonstrate a real connection with tech and as such, the real estate returns might take a bit of a backseat. As I said, these aren't traditional venues for a real estate investor to look for financing, but you never know what sort of an idea might attract people.

Take the time to review whether any of these accelerator programs might be a fit for you. If they aren't and if you're solely interested in traditional real estate projects, then feel free to ignore them.

Private Equity Firms

There are multiple ways in which you could go with this. You could set up your own private equity fund and source investment funding from those close to you and then eventually from outside investors. The other option is to directly approach institutions that are active in this area.

In order to get in touch with these institutions, it's best to know someone who is close to the principal of the firm. One of the best ways to do this is to do some searching online. Search for private equity real estate investment funds and firms and you'll receive a list of them.

You can conduct this search on LinkedIn as well. Search for these firms' company pages and look at the list of employees. If you happen to spot someone who happens to be known to someone else in your network, you could ask for an introduction. Keep their portfolio size in mind when evaluating them as potential investors.

These firms manage hundreds of millions of dollars and as a result, the deal sizes they look at tend to be in the millions. The other thing to keep in mind is that these firms are used to operating the deals by themselves. As someone who brings the deal in without equity, a finder's fee is about all you can hope for.

However, a 5% fee on a million dollar deal is $50,000, which is more than enough to get you started on your own smaller deals. So don't brush this away too soon. In order to connect with these people, you'll have to gain an introduction from someone close to them.

Typically, they will not respond to LinkedIn mail or messages. You could try to source their emails using software such as Hunter.io and cold email them, but the odds of them replying to you are low. Smaller funds might be interested but it's hit or miss. Look at some industry events that are coming up and see if you can attend these.

Such events are great places to network with these people, and you can pitch your deal to them. You'll have to work on your pitch quite a bit in order to get noticed, but if the deal goes through, you'll likely end up with enough money that you can use to fund your own business.

If you decide to go down the route of opening your own fund, you'll need to have a ton of expertise in this field and you certainly won't need me to tell you where to look for funds. As such, I'm not going to address this route.

Networking and engaging with your connections is the key to sourcing interest from real estate investors. Position yourself as an authority and a credible voice in the subject, and you'll find that you'll be able to gain their interest. The private equity option is best pursued if you happen to source an extremely large deal that you can't take advantage of personally.

In such cases, see if you can gain some equity in the deal. This will result in a windfall for you, and you won't have to do much work to obtain these gains. If not, then even a finder's fee should do the trick and get you started down the road to profitable real estate investment of your own.

A subset of the private equity investing class that often gets ignored are mortgage notes investors. These investors buy delinquent mortgages on properties, and thanks to the state of default these notes are in, they end up financing physical real estate at some point.

They also happen more to smaller investors compared to private equity firms. Look up mortgage notes investing online. There are a ton of resources on the subject, such as Notes School and Biggerpockets. There are also a number of channels that are dedicated to explaining how the process works.

Since these investors are used to playing the bank in their investments, they might be open to financing a deal and in being your bank. Developing relationships and establishing trust is the key since they won't know who you are. What's more, they probably receive a ton of pitches every day, so take the time to get introduced to them or connect with them in person if possible.

It might take time to develop these relationships, but with perseverance you'll get there!

Chapter 4:

How to Ask for Money

The thing about trying to raise money is that, at some point, you're going to have to ask for it. This causes a lot of discomfort for a lot of people. Most of us are raised with certain unhealthy beliefs about money. Given its importance in our lives, these beliefs play a central role in how we perceive its existence and how we deal with it.

Asking for money is a minefield because it's easy for us to project our insecurities onto the situation and come across as being insincere in our request. You might think you're being respectful by not talking about the exact amount of money you need, but this could be misperceived as a lack of confidence by your investor.

Putting yourself in the shoes of your potential investors isn't a technique that works too well either. After all, it's your beliefs that are creating the issue. No matter how many shoes you wear, you're going to keep carrying them inside your head. This chapter is going to simplify this process and give you an actionable template that you can use to figure out how to ask for money.

Given the one-size fits-all nature of a template, you might have to switch a few things around. Before we get into the details of asking for money, understand that a lot of successful fundraising is simply all about avoiding mistakes. Don't do the things that will cost you money or investors, and this will put you in a good position to actually receive it.

Why is this true? Well, the truth is that most of us are uncomfortable talking about money. Even the most financially secure among us. Try walking up to a rich looking person who works a regular job and ask them how much they make per year. Then watch them squirm or become hostile towards you.

Your investors are probably slightly uncomfortable with the process as well, and have been through the experience you're now undergoing. They'll want to make it easy for you to ask them for an amount. However, you're the one that needs to ask. You can't expect people to simply write you a check through hints and glances that you've been delivering them.

Get comfortable uttering the words "I want $xyz..." and so on. Repeat it to yourself every day, whenever you can, stand in front of a mirror and say it out loud. You'll find that with practice, a lot of the shyness and discomfort around the topic will disappear.

Once you have a good handle over your discomfort, understand that you don't need to do anything special. Keep it simple and straightforward. That's more than enough for you to be able to raise all the money you need. Don't try to put on any airs or try to rope people in through specially designed marketing spiels.

Stick to the facts surrounding your deal and trust that you'll attract the right people to you. There's a very good reason for you to do this. Remember that a lot of capital raising is about successfully screening the right types of investors into your circle of opportunity.

If you're going to rely on sales heavy pitches that make used car salesmen blush, you're going to attract people who focus on that sort of thing and not on the serious money making bit. This is especially true in the case of angel investors. Social media is awash with people calling themselves investors when they don't have any money to invest.

What they're really looking for is information on your deal that they can then resell to other people, and take a cut from you. The best way to screen such people out is to stick to the facts and tell them exactly what you're looking for. Give them your elevator pitch when asked and gauge their response.

If they don't wish to go into details and immediately promise you money, run for the hills. They either don't know what they're doing or they're trying to shop your deal around to other people. By sticking to the facts and not worrying about sales pitches, you'll manage to attract the right people to you.

So with all of that being said, let's now jump in and look at how you can determine how much you need to ask off your investors.

How Much?

You can't ask for money unless you know how much you want. This is a problem that a lot of investors run into. They run the numbers long and hard, but are still not sure of how much money they'll need. Ask for too little and you'll come across as amateurish. Ask for too much and you'll be seen as greedy.

The best-case scenario when you ask for the incorrect amount is that you'll be viewed as incompetent, which is not a good look. Here are the factors you need to take into account in order to ask for the right amount of money.

Cost of Capital

All capital costs money. As head-spinning as that sentence sounds, it's pretty simple in spirit. Nothing is free. The angel investor who gives you money expects equity in return down the road. The conventional lender that gives you money expects interest payments every month. Hard money lenders want interest and a balloon payment at the end of the term. Your great uncle Bob expects you to not screw up or no more Thanksgiving turkey for you!

Every source of capital has associated costs. You'll need to pay for lawyers to draft agreements. You'll need to pay closing costs if using a conventional loan and so on. These costs play an important role in your decision-making process. Generally, it makes sense to choose the cheapest source of capital.

However, consider that costs can be qualitative as well. A mortgage might have high closing costs, but it certainly comes with a lot more traditional support. It doesn't cost you any equity. If something goes wrong, you have an established framework of professionals to turn and ask questions to.

This might not be the case if you choose to run an investment partnership with your friends and family's money pooled into it. Consider costs from all angles. It helps to write down the pros and cons of all options available to you. Pick the one that has the least number of negatives or has the negative you can live with.

When done this way, you might find that your initial assumption about some source of capital might not be the most efficient, and that a seemingly higher cost of capital offers advantages that cheaper capital doesn't. Do not try to shortcut this process. Sit down and write everything down and don't rush through this in a few minutes.

Your Portfolio and Deal

This one is fairly simple to figure out. The bigger the portfolio you're looking to finance, the more money you'll need. You'll need to list all of the costs of the project line-wise, and estimate costs. Let's use a home flip deal as an example. The first cost you'll need to list is the interest cost or cost of capital.

Most banks do not finance flippers. You'll have to approach a wealthy investor and give them equity, or you'll need to find a hard money lender. Most investors choose the latter option since interest is cheaper from a qualitative standpoint. You'll pay more upfront and the debt burden is a pain, but you get to keep all profits.

Next, you'll need to list the ownership costs. You're not going to flip this overnight. In order to extract maximum value, you're going to have to hang onto the property for a while. You could even consider placing it on rent if this is the case. Given the restrictions around FHA financing, you'll have to wait for at least six to seven months.

This depends on the area you're selling your home, of course. If it happens to be in a price range that someone with great credit can afford to finance from a conventional lender, then you could place it on sale after two months or so. Generally, it's best to budget for six months to a year since you want to account for the worst-case scenario.

Ownership costs include utilities, maintenance costs and property taxes. If the place remains vacant during this time, this is also a cost. I'll shortly explain how to account for this. Add the ownership costs that you can figure out and record them.

Next up are the deal implementation costs. This is a flipper, so you're going to have to put work into fixing it. How much will this cost? This is a tricky thing to estimate. A contractor is not going to give you the exact quote unless they're certain you've secured financing to buy the place. As a first time investor, no contractor is going to do you a favor and take time out of their day and not get paid for it.

So how should you figure out costs? The simplest way is to be meticulous when inspecting the property. Take pictures of everything and take lots of notes. Ask the seller for property information and record everything they say. You could persuade a contractor you have a good relationship with to sit down with you over a coffee and take a look at what you have.

Alternatively, you could drive to the nearest Home Depot or Lowe's and speak to the salespeople there. All of them tend to be former contractors or part-time handymen. They'll have a fairly good idea of how much the repair work will cost. Use your contacts online to estimate repairs.

Now that all of this is done, you'll need to add these repairs up and add a 10% buffer to that to account for unexpected delays. You can now use this number to figure out how much you need to offer the seller. There's a very simple rule of thumb to do this.

The first step is to estimate the ARV. You can get this by looking at home listings or simply asking the agent connected to the property. Subtract the repair costs from this number. Offer 70% of this value.

If the ARV is $200,000 and the repairs will cost you $6,000, you should offer no more than 70% of $194,000 which is $135,800. This will give you a nice buffer in case things go wrong.

Next, you'll need to figure out the NOI from the property. Look at the market rate for rentals in the area and use this figure. Now halve this number. This will be your NOI. This is the 50% rule of real estate. Use this number to account for property ownership costs from the earlier step.

To sum up, you now have your ideal offer price, your projected return (thanks to the ARV) and the monthly cash flow you'll incur thanks to owning the property. Put all of this together into your pitch deck. If you're going for conventional financing, you'll need 20% of your offer price.

If you feel you won't qualify for this and will have to go down the hard money route, you'll need 40% of that price as a down payment. This amounts to $54,320. Let's say you have just $10,000 in your bank account for this deal. This leaves $44,320 to be raised from a private investor on an equity basis and the rest to be provided by the hard money lender.

When presenting your cash outflows to the private investor, remember to subtract the hard money interest from the NOI. The 50% rule does not take the mortgage interest into account.

Clarify Return on Investment

ROI is what your private investor is going to be looking at. They'll specifically be looking for the cap rate and the cash-on-cash return. The cap rate is the NOI divided by the price of the property (the ARV). You want this to be in line with the prevalent cap rates in the area.

You'll receive this information from the agent or even through online research. Let's say your NOI from the property is $1,000 per month. This works out to $12,000 per year. If the property is valued at $150,000 your cap rate is eight percent. Compare this to the prevalent rates in the area to check whether you're maximizing revenues from your property.

The cap rate also explains why raising rents is normal practice. As the property's value increases, the cap rate decreases if NOI remains the same. Thus, raising rents is standard practice. You want to take affordability into account as well. In some areas, it might be better to keep rents the same and ensure long tenancy instead of trying to maximize cap rates.

The area's demographics should inform this decision, and you should make a note of it in your pitch deck.

If you plan on selling the property back into the market, then capital gains will be the primary driver of returns. Using the numbers from the previous example, your purchase price was $135,800 and the ARV was $200,000. The repairs cost you $6,000. Thus, the total investment in the property is $141,800.

Assuming you receive a selling price of $200,000, that's a capital gain of 41% on the property, which is massive. You will need to subtract interest costs from this number since you've opted for a hard money purchase. Since the loan is interest-only and the loan amount is $81,480 (you and your private investor have 40% equity in the deal), and since the interest is assumed to be 15% of the loan amount per year, you'll incur a yearly interest expense of $12,122.

This is the expense you'll realize if you hang onto the property for an entire year. If you manage to sell it within six months, it'll be around half that amount. Let's make it simple and assume you own the property for this long. Thus, your interest expense is $6,111.

Your costs of buying the property now amount to the purchase price, the repair costs and the interest expense. This reduces your capital gains to 35% which is still an astronomical return.

These numbers are absolute returns on the capital deployed on the purchase. What will be your own return and that of your investor's? They've invested $44,320 in the project and you've invested $10,000. Collectively the two of you own 40% of the deal. Your stake amounts to 18% of the profits, and theirs amounts to 82%.

You calculate this by figuring out how much equity the two of you own in the overall deal. Of the 40%, you own 7%, and they own 33%. The lender owns the rest. However, the lender doesn't get a cut of the profits since they're being paid interest. Therefore, the owners of the 40% get full access to it. Since you own 7% of the overall deal, you control 18% of the 40% and your investor controls 82% of the 40% (7/40 and 33/40 respectively).

Let's assume all expenses are borne on a 50/50 basis between the two of you. This means the repair costs of $6,000 and interest expense of $6,111 are shared equally. This increases the cash investment in the deal from both parties to around $6,000 each. You've now invested $16,000, and they've invested $50,320 in the project.

The returns from the deal amount to a total of $52,089. You get 18% of this number which is $9,376.02. Your investor receives the rest which is $42,712.98.

Your ROI is equal to this return divided by the cash you invested in the project. This is equal to an 58.6% return (9376.02/16000) and your investor's cash on cash return (ROI) is 84%.

All of these numbers might seem like too much to deal with. This is because you've read of all of them at once. Work the numbers of your deal in a step by step manner and you'll see that they aren't that difficult to work out. It's just that, if you take in all of them at once, they'll be overwhelming.

With regard to the cost expenditure in this deal, remember that the hard money lender might lend you an amount that is based on the ARV of the property. In this example, I've assumed for simplicity's sake that they're lending you 60% of the purchase price. However, if they lend you 60% of the ARV, you and your investor won't need to spend money on repairs since this additional amount will cover those expenses.

You will incur higher interest costs, but the higher returns you make on the deal will compensate for this.

Itemize Expenses

If you happen to receive more money than you planned for, it can be easy to go overboard and spend all of it. This is why it's extremely important to itemize all of your expenses and clarify to your investor how their money is going to be spent. Doing this will also help you develop a clear path as to how you're going to spend the money you'll receive.

Plan for expenditures ahead of time so that you don't find yourself in a position where you'll need to explain to your investor why you need more money. It's a good idea to add a buffer of 10% to your calculations when asking them for money. This gives you some leeway in case the unexpected happens.

Depending on the type of deal, you might need to increase this buffer. Rehabs are notorious for unearthing additional costs. You might want to set aside a 20% buffer in this case. It comes down to how uncertain the costs are for your individual project. Don't be afraid to ask your investor whether your numbers make sense.

If they happen to have a lot of experience in these deals, then using their input to come up with better numbers will make them trust you more. Appearing to know everything and pretending that your numbers are infallible is a great way to lose money.

The Process of Asking

So you've figured out your numbers and now the time has come to go ahead and ask them for the cash. How does one do this exactly? This is usually the most nerve wracking part of the process. Here are a few tips that will help you ace the process.

Focus on Quality

Pitching is nerve wracking and it takes a lot of energy. Not only do you have to deal with the objections of the person you're pitching to, you'll need to deal with your own nerves as well. Some novices decide to make their pitches grandiose and flowery. This is a mistake.

If you happen to be nervous about the process, it's best to simplify things. This way you won't have additional things to worry about when the time comes. You'll be able to react better in real time to their questions and your natural creativity and charisma will shine through.

Above all else, simplicity works because it reduces your presentation or pitch down to its best quality. By stripping it of all things that are non-essential, you get your prospective investor to focus on the most important parts of your deal. This is what the investor wants as well.

They're busy people and probably receive tons of pitches every day. They want to quickly figure out whether a deal is worth their time or not. This is why creating an elevator pitch is so helpful. It condenses the best points of your deal quickly, and in a minute, it helps you investors figure out whether it's worth it or not.

Don't try to build up too much intrigue or try to copy write your way through this. Marketing is not what you're aiming for here. Be genuine and highlight how great your deal is. Focus on the numbers once your prospective investor is interested. Walk them through the specifics of the deal.

Use the 90/10 method I previously mentioned. Explain 90% of the deal's important points, and let them ask you questions about the remaining 10%. Don't leave important information out or else you'll look uninformed or naive. Instead, leave out some of the minor costs as you explain the numbers to them. This way, they'll ask you questions and will engage with you a lot more.

Focus on the realistic nature of your numbers. Don't assume the best or worst-case scenarios. Instead, land somewhere in the middle. It also helps to prepare a worst-case scenario. By doing this, you can show them what the numbers would look like in case everything goes wrong. This will also set a return baseline in the investors' minds and you'll find them warming up to your deal.

Above all else, focus on attracting the right investors to you instead of trying to force people to come on board. Think of it as you setting a table full of tasty dishes that people will feel compelled to try, as opposed to walking around trying to shove your food into their mouths. The latter is what many desperate real estate entrepreneurs do.

Don't be one of them.

Keep it Succinct

Know what the point is and stick to it. This is a business presentation and not a marketing one. Skip the fancy graphics if you're presenting electronically. Stay away from buzzwords like 'synergies' and 'entropies' or whatever advertisers talk about these days.

Instead, explain the terms of the deal in plain language that everyone can understand. This is a great way of filtering for investors who you will get along well with. An investor that focuses on the deal and on its numbers will be a lot easier to work with. This is because their focus is in the right place.

A novice investor who has money but doesn't have the emotional maturity to handle it will resort to personal attacks when things start going wrong. They'll blame you for mishandling the project, even if the situation was out of your control. They'll play the victim and will behave as if their world has come crashing down.

What's more they'll land themselves in trouble sooner or later because they'll end up risking way too much on their business deals. You'll be guilt tripped into thinking that you've played a part in their demise. It's best to stay away from such emotional vampires.

A great way of identifying such people is to watch for their reaction when they talk about the market or their investment experience. A high frequency of buzzwords and stories that are light on details is a dead giveaway. If possible, take a look at some of the people they've worked with on their deals. If these people are nothing like you, or conform to the worst stereotypes I just listed, stay away from them.

Many entrepreneurs forget that asking for money is a two-way street. You're asking for money, but you're also providing access to something valuable in exchange for that money. What you have to offer is just as valuable to the investor as their money is to you. This is why you want to attract the right investor, not just any schlep with money in their pocket.

To do this, present a business-like manner and don't stray away from the important points of your deal. The details of your deal are the most important parts of it, and a good investor will focus on this. The inexperienced investor will focus instead of things such as the top-line profit and the different things you could do to boost that number.

A desirable investor will instead focus on the risk inherent in the deal and will ask you questions about how you plan on mitigating it. For example, in the flipping deal we looked at recently, the good investor will ask you about your plans for financing if the hard money lender doesn't come through or lends you a lot less than you imagined.

Will you sell more equity in the deal? Will you raise money from family and friends? They'll also quiz you about timelines. What if the property doesn't sell for months on end? What is your strategy then? How will you attract high-quality tenants to the property and how long will this take to bear fruit?

At first they will seem pessimistic, and your confidence in the positives of the deal is likely to be tested.

However, if you pass these tests, you're not only likely to receive money, but you'll end up making them a source of investment you can keep returning to with more deals.

So always focus on the details and keep it short and sweet. Don't simplify your deal but don't complicate it either. Make it as complex as it needs to be. A good investor will appreciate this effort.

Realistic Numbers

This ties in with the general theme of these tips. Don't exaggerate your revenue projections or underestimate your costs, an experienced investor will spot these from a mile away. While it's acceptable to use numbers that are on the optimistic side of things, overdoing this to a point of irrationality is a red flag.

For example, if the cap rate of a neighborhood is eight percent, and if your deal projects a cap rate of 16%, this is ridiculous. There is no way you'll ever manage to double the existing cap rate on a property in a neighborhood. After all, the other landlords aren't uninformed enough to settle for such numbers.

Many entrepreneurs seeking funding tend to exaggerate their numbers in a bid to make it seem as if they've found a diamond that has been hidden in plain sight. Such things do happen, but the diamonds aren't as exaggerated as what most novices think. Instead of trying to shoot the lights out with your deal, aim to generate consistent returns.

This is the hallmark of a high-quality deal. Remember that quality investors are a lot more concerned with the consistency of numbers and with the risks inherent in the deal. You can tout 500% returns in your elevator pitch, but once the details are looked into there might be huge risks involved.

Besides, if your real estate deal could really generate 500% returns, there's no way a sensible person would ever offer someone else equity in it. They'd likely seek bank debt to fund the deal. This is just common sense. So don't exaggerate your numbers. Prepare projections for the worst-case scenario, but don't highlight them unless the investor asks for it.

Be realistic with your projections and costs and you'll find that serious investors will flock to you.

Be Mature

Some people take rejection way too harshly and end up scuppering their chances even more. Rejection is hard to handle, and it is tough to hear the word "no" after having put so much work into your deal. However, if you want to get anywhere with your deal, you're going to have to hear this many times over.

Some entrepreneurs keep chasing the investor in the hopes of getting their no answer overturned. If you've given them all the details about your deal and have still not managed to pique their interest, nothing more you say is going to do the job. Thank them for their time and ask them whether there's a way you can stay in touch with them in case something else comes up.

This method of asking to remain in touch is the best way to build a network of investors, even if the current deal didn't work out. It puts the investor at ease since they know that you're a mature business person and not a child who has just had its candy taken away from him.

From the investor's perspective saying no is hard as well. They're looking to place their money in profitable deals. They want your project and your pitch to captivate them as much as you want it to. They're just as disappointed when it doesn't work out. Saying "no" is hard because they understand that they're disappointing someone. No one wakes up in the morning looking forward to doing this.

So make it easy for them to handle the situation. Show them you're a mature person and that this isn't the only deal you have going on. By asking for permission to stay in touch, you're telling them that you have other opportunities in the pipeline and that you are active in this space.

If they warm up to you but still reject the deal, ask them for feedback on what the issue is. Perhaps there's some problem that you haven't spotted? Or perhaps you've been underestimating some risk parameter? Gathering feedback like this not only helps refine your pitch, it also helps you understand what they're looking for.

This boosts your chances of receiving an investment from them in the future. Above all else, do not assume the stance of begging for money. You don't "have to" have their money. Don't get so carried away with your deal that you come to believe it's the opportunity of a lifetime. Very few such instances occur in life, and the odds of a novice unearthing such things are close to zero. So settle down and don't take things personally.

Mistakes to Avoid

As I mentioned earlier, a lot of successful real estate capital raising is all about avoiding the things that can sabotage your success. Don't make these silly mistakes and you'll manage to raise all the money you need.

Ignoring Feedback

This ties in with the final tip in the previous section. While you want to source high-quality investment funds into your deal, you should also be on the lookout for feedback from these sources. If you find that only low-quality investors that focus on the unrealistic side of things are getting attracted to your deal, you're obviously doing something wrong.

Often, good investors will provide you with feedback if you seem sincere about your deal's merits. These investors usually look to help up-and-comers succeed, and if you show them that you're open to feedback, they will give it to you. They'll clearly state what the deal's weak points are and what problems you'll face.

At this point, most entrepreneurs turn around and argue with these investors. They think it's a debate when really, it's a lesson. Even if you disagree with their points or feel it's not relevant, thank them for their feedback and time. Most people don't go around providing help, so understand the value of receiving such feedback.

Arguing or trying to prove them wrong doesn't achieve anything. For one thing, you'll only frustrate them and make them regret they gave you advice. Second, they'll cross you off their list of promising deal makers. They might not be right with regard to your deal, but there's no need to for you to prove this.

Take an honest look at your deal's points and evaluate whether they're right or wrong. It takes courage to do this. However, don't fool yourself into thinking you know everything. Take feedback and receive it with grace when you get it.

Exaggerating the Cash You Need

While underestimating the amount of cash you need is a common mistake, exaggerating the amount that you need is an even bigger one. I'm not talking about building adequate buffers into your projections. I'm referring to assuming unrealistic cash flow requirements that make no sense whatsoever.

Even if your intentions are sincere, check to see whether your numbers make sense. Going to serious investors with these kinds of numbers will get you laughed out of the room. You'll lose credibility instantly, and it's unlikely that investors will ever want to work with you again.

From an investor's standpoint, there are just two explanations for such behavior. The first is that you're clueless, which is bad. The second is that you're dishonest and are trying to pocket some excess cash, which is way worse. Either way you're not someone who can be trusted with their money.

Run your numbers past a few experts in the field. If you're running a flip, run your cost estimates past a few contractors, either in person or online. Run it past other investors you've networked with and solicit feedback. This is a great way to approach investors you already know but have rejected you in the past.

Tell them you're working on a deal and would love their feedback on it. Run a few numbers past them to see what they think. Whether they get hooked onto this deal is immaterial. Your objective is to build your relationship with them and to remain in touch. If they ask for more numbers, then show them your proposal.

Making Unrealistic Demands

You're willing to put just $5,000 in cash on an equity stake worth $100,000, but want 90% of the profits. This kind of thing is a scenario many investors encounter more often than you think. Unrealistic demands are the easiest way to get laughed at, some investors will even react with hostility because it's downright disrespectful to offer such terms.

Many novice entrepreneurs do this unknowingly because they simply don't understand how money and risk works. If you aren't willing to put up any equity in a deal, but still want an even split on the profits, you're not going to get it. I've already mentioned how a finder's fee or sweat equity with 15% is all you can hope for.

Did this offend you in some way? Did you think you're the one doing all the work and the investor is the one pocketing all the profit? If your answer is yes, then frankly, you don't understand how money works. The investor is the one absorbing all the risk on such a deal. You might be doing the running around but if the deal doesn't work, you've not lost any money.

So examine what you're bringing to the table in terms of risk exposure. It isn't just about doing all the work. You need to expose yourself to risk, as well, in order to see some sort of a stake in the profits in the deal.

Not Respecting Their Time

Many entrepreneurs rock up to investors and expect them to provide all of their knowledge for free or on the spot. They think they can simply keep asking questions of them and receive answers in return. It doesn't work this way. You need to respect their time in order to get them to listen to you or even consider your deal.

If you're young, then you might get away with simply showing up and asking them questions. Most experienced investors are willing to help college-aged or younger people. However, you can't keep doing this all the time. A better way to have your questions answered is to approach them and seek time for an informational interview.

This way, you're showing them that you respect their time and are conscious of not wasting it. The same principle applies when you're pitching to them. Make sure your numbers make sense, and that you're clear with regard to all of the information you wish to highlight.

Try to anticipate all of their questions and prepare answers to them. You don't need to blow them away with the extent of your preparation. Simply demonstrating that you've taken care to present your deal and yourself in the best manner possible will be more than enough.

After all, they've taken time out of their busy day to give you attention. Respect this act by showing that you care as well. Don't behave as if your deal is the best in the world and that they should be privileged enough to sit at the same table as you.

Focusing on the Wrong Things

In the interest of covering all bases, some entrepreneurs begin focusing on irrelevant details. This is just a waste of time. For example, if you're seeking investment for a flipper, then focusing on the breakdown between the cost of painting the property between two service providers is not really needed.

This just shows you don't know what is important to the deal's bottom line and that you're trying to deflect attention away from the more important things. Your investors will hear alarm bells ringing when they see this kind of thing happening, so take care to avoid it.

It's great that you have an eye for detail, but there's no need to bore your investors with every single detail there is.

Using Boilerplates

If you've been approaching different investors then you'll be tempted to use the same script with them over and over. This saves you time and will help you approach more investors in a shorter span of time. It will also end up potentially offending your prospective investors.

You're seeking money from someone and a substantial amount of it. If you approach each and every person with the same spiel, then you're only ensuring that your pitch doesn't fit any single person's criteria or preferences.

Instead, take the time to get to know your investors. Look at what kinds of deals they're in the market for, and get to know what they prefer in deals in terms of structure. Every investor is different. Your job is to tailor your pitch to each and every single individual you come across.

This isn't as hard as it sounds. More often than not, people will tell you what they want. It's your job to simply listen to them and tailor your pitch accordingly. If an investor tells you right off the bat they're interested only in development deals and not in flipping homes, don't pitch your deal to them (assuming it isn't a property development project.)

Communicate with them according to their preferences. You're the one asking for money after all. This is the least you could so.

Being Less Than Honest

This is a big one. Throughout this book I've been stressing how important it is to be honest in your communication with your investors. You need to be upfront about the numbers in your deal and also honest about the risks inherent in it. You need to do this to attract the right kinds of investors as well as build credibility.

Being honest is just good business. It'll help you form long-lasting business relationships with people, and you won't need to worry about finding new investors on every single deal you encounter.

Be honest and you'll find that you'll need to search for investors just once or twice. Once you manage to earn profits from a deal, you'll find that your existing investors will introduce you to other people who are looking to deploy their capital as well, and you'll manage to attract capital to you.

Chapter 5:

How to Structure Deals and

Partnerships

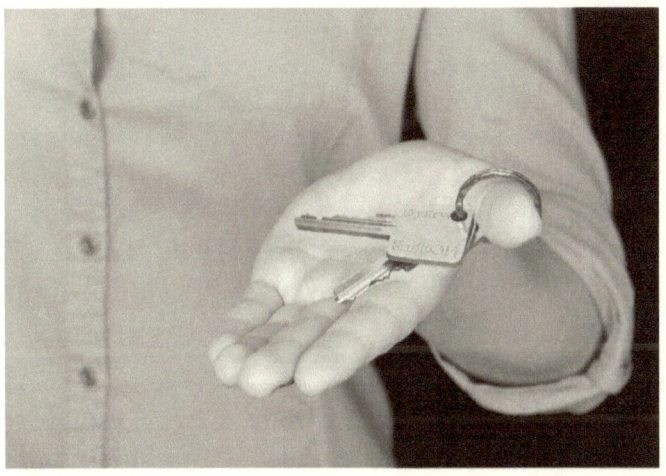

You've learned all about how to clarify the financial aspects of your deals. It's now time to look at the legal structure of your deals. Truth be told, consulting an experienced real estate attorney is your best move in this regard. However, it pays to understand what sort of legal structures are available for you to use, and how each one functions.

Why do you even need a legal structure in the first place? Well, this should be pretty obvious. Not only do you want to protect your investor's money, you want to protect yourself from liability and other claims that might result from the property. Let's begin by taking a look at the simplest legal structure there is.

Sole Proprietorships

These are the simplest legal entities out there and require almost no paperwork to file. You can literally roll out of bed and begin operating as a sole proprietor. Contrary to popular perception, you can conduct business through agents or employees while a sole proprietor. It means filing some additional paperwork come tax-time, but it really isn't too much of a headache.

The obvious downside to this legal entity is that you cannot raise money or give someone equity in your deals if you're conducting business. To do this, you will need to use one of the other entities mentioned in this chapter.

Having said that, if you have enough cash raised from a previous deal or are looking to collect a finder's fee from bringing a deal to an investor, then this is a good option for you to pursue. Something to keep in mind is that the business will be conducted in your own name and as a result, you will be liable for all damages or actions that you carry out.

For example, if a tenant injures themselves in your property and decides to sue you in court, all of your assets are on-the-line since they aren't legally protected.

General Partnerships

If you wish to keep things less formal but still want to be able to invest in properties using the help of an outside equity investor, then a general partnership presents the least number of hassles. All states have different laws but generally speaking, the differences boil down to a few nuances.

A general partnership in some states doesn't even require any legal agreements to be filed or any form of incorporation to have taken place (*Choice of Entity Considerations for Real Estate Investors,* 2020). For example, in California a general partnership can be formed verbally between consent parties.

Advantages

The biggest advantage is the complete lack of hassle in terms of paperwork and filing requirements. You're entering into a private agreement with another person and you decide to split the profits accordingly. Typically, people opting for a general partnership use a 50/50 structure, but this is merely the default option.

You can use any structure that suits you. If you happen to know your investor very well and are on good personal terms with them, then introducing legalities might be counterproductive. In such situations, a general partnership is a good vehicle to use.

Disadvantages

You and your partners are not protected from liabilities arising from your properties. Furthermore, this method only works if you happen to know and trust your investment partners well. If they happen to be close friends or family, this method might work. However, approaching a third-party investor with this structure in mind will come across as being unprofessional.

In such cases, it makes a lot more sense to look at some of the other options presented. When it comes to general partnerships, you cannot designate a single person as being the one who will manage the property. Every partner has equal rights when it comes to running and managing the property.

This means that in case of disputes, you might have a huge problem on your hands.

Limited Partnerships

The limited partnership combines the benefits of the general partnership and the fact that partners can enjoy full liability protection. Under this legal agreement, the limited partners can passively enjoy their share of the profits from the investment without being exposed to any liability beyond their initial investment.

There is a downside to this agreement, though. Typically, limited partnerships (LP) designate an entity to be a general partner (GP) and it is this partner that carries out the day-to-day operations of the LP. This structure is best suited for people who don't wish to assume an active role in investment and wish to create passive income.

Advantages

The biggest advantage you can offer to your investors is the fact that they can simply sit back and collect profits from the deal. They won't have to worry about running the show day to day. Instead, you as the GP do all the work, and they get to collect the results of that work.

The lack of liability exposure also is a huge advantage for LPs. Investors who have a ton of property investments usually won't have the time to keep track of every single detail pertaining to them. It's far easier for them to invest in deals structured in this way.

If you're looking to raise funds through friends and family, this structure works very well. As the LPs, they agree to leave you in charge and collect their share of the profits.

Disadvantages

Some investors wish to assume a more active role in their deals and want the legal protection to be able to do this. An LP structure doesn't give them this. As the GP, you can legally overrule them, and they won't have any grounds to withdraw their money. A disagreement between the LP and the GP will result in less protection for the former party.

As a result, some angel investors won't agree to this structure and might suggest an alternative. If you happen to be pitching this structure, then your reputation and expertise will count for a lot since you'll be the one running the show. Thus, there is a chance of your relative inexperience overshadowing the attractiveness of the deals you're investing in.

Limited Liability Company

A limited liability company, or an LLC, is one of the most common forms of incorporation in the United States. The premise of this legal structure is simple. The LLC acts as a standalone entity only for business purposes. The earnings are passed directly to the owner of the LLC.

However, the liability associated with the property stops at the LLC's level. It is an extremely flexible structure to own, and in most cases, you don't need a separate bank account to operate the company. Do keep in mind that if you don't separate your finances from the LLC's, your assets will be assumed to be that of the LLC's and as a result, you'll lose liability protection.

When it comes to bringing other people on board, the LLC offers a pretty straightforward path. The articles of incorporation need to be amended with the state where the company is incorporated in. The ownership share of the people who come on board can be determined by either their financial contribution or on the basis of services rendered.

This is not the case with the LP, where everyone typically needs to have a financial stake in the structure.

Advantages

The LLC is extremely flexible when it comes to determining ownership structure. What's more, individual members of the LLC can be designated as managing partners or not. This means an LLC can have multiple partners who are designated as such and have a say over how the day-to-day operations of the LLC are managed.

This can provide solace to investors who wish to have a greater say in the way their investments are managed. Investors that simply wish to collect their checks passively can be designated as non-managing members. Thus, the LLC solves everyone's issues elegantly.

The members of the LLC are free to reassign their interests in the LLC to parties of their choice. While custom is to seek the approval of other members in the LLC, the legal hurdles of transferring their ownership share to someone else is extremely low with LLCs. This is not the case with other legal structures.

Over and above all this is the fact that liability is limited to what every member has invested in the LLC. In the case of an LP, the GP's personal assets can be held to account, but this is not the case with an LLC.

Disadvantages

While there are many advantages of an LLC, there are a few disadvantages as well. For starters, you will need to separate all legal and financial records of the LLC from your own in order to obtain the full benefits of the liability protection. If you happen to run the business or say collect rent checks, in your personal account, you've just exposed all of your assets to liability claims.

The LLC has a number of ongoing costs that an LP or a general partnership doesn't have. You will need to file tax records with the IRS every January, whether you made money or not, and this will cost you the services of a professional CPA. Your own tax preparation will become a little more complex thanks to the LLC's pass-through structure, and this might cost you more money.

Some entrepreneurs prefer to incorporate as an S-Corp because of the increased possibility of saving taxes. LLCs cost around as much to form, and if your business is earning significant amounts of cash, this might not be the best structure to do business under.

Corporations

There are two types of corporations that one can form in the United States. One is called a C-corp, while the other is an S-corp. S-corps are the ones that are used more frequently, while C-corps are typically used by international investors. The S-corp offers investors huge tax advantages, but it does come at additional cost.

While forming an S-corp is as straightforward as starting an LLC, there are running costs to take into account. An S-corp requires full-time accounting services since these companies will usually have to pay an estimated amount of tax every month to the IRS. This is not the case with an LLC.

The S-corp is a full-fledged entity on its own and needs to be treated as such. This means it is liable to pay corporate taxes, and needs to have an elected board of directors and officers in charge. You will be liable for personal taxes on the salary you draw from the company. You can also sell shares in the company and treat this income as capital gains.

Alternatively, you could simply leave the capital in the company and buy more shares in the structure, thereby reducing your personal taxes to next to nothing. S-corps also give you the opportunity to deduct a lot of expenses and as a result, you'll end up saving more in terms of taxes.

Given the high running costs, it's best to seek the advice of a CPA before forming one. If your revenues are not over a certain threshold, it might not make sense to form one.

Advantages

The tax reduction possibilities offer the biggest advantage of an S-corp structure. There is also little chance of liability hitting you personally since the company is deemed an entity by itself. This gives you the best possible separation between your personal assets and the ones owned by your company.

You can elect officers to serve as managers of the company and these people do not need to be shareholders. Thus, if you ever wish to step aside and make your real estate investments passive, you can hire someone else to run the show in your place. Bringing new investors on board is simply a matter of issuing shares at the relevant price.

This makes tracking equity interests in the company easy. If a member wishes to exit, all they have to do is sell their shares and their ownership can be absorbed by the rest of the shareholders in the company.

Disadvantages

An S-corp costs time and money to administer. This is why it doesn't make sense for new investors to incorporate in this manner. You will need to have a good level of cash flow to be able to pay for the expenses that you will incur. You will need to conduct board meetings and record notes for those meetings and so on.

In some cases, if you don't have enough investors on board, the separation between the entity and yourself could blur. There is legal precedent for this in the state of California (*Choice of Entity Considerations for Real Estate Investors*, 2020). In those cases, the liability was massive, and there weren't enough shareholders in the company for management to claim credibly that they were separate entities from the business.

As such, their liability protection was overturned. This is something to be wary of if you don't have enough investors on board.

Partnership Agreements

At the end of the day, you're going to have to strike a deal with your partners and will have to agree to certain terms. Ensuring that your partnership agreement contains the right language and hits the important points is crucial. This will let your investor rest in ease that they're protected and makes sure that both of your rights are safeguarded.

Here are the important sections that your agreement needs to address at all costs.

Roles

If you're going to be the one who will absorb all the tasks related to ensuring the deal is executed, then this section will be pretty short. However, most deals involve investor input in terms of sales and marketing. In some instances, they could even contribute their services to ensure the deal goes through.

If this is the case, you should take the time to clearly state who does what. This is even more critical if there are multiple partners involved in the deal.

Financials

This section doesn't refer to the financials of the deal, but rather to the investment made by each partner and the amount of equity they own in the deal. It should clearly state how expenses will be accounted for, in what proportion and how the profits will be divided. It's also a good idea to describe exactly what a profit is and how it'll be calculated (Merrill, 2020a).

This might seem a trivial thing to do, but in reality it helps avoid a ton of conflict down the road.

Commitment

How much of your time will either of you spend on this deal? If one of you has a full-time job then it's important to clearly mention the time commitment that each party will bring to the deal. Discussing this beforehand is helpful in determining who gets what proportion of the company.

In some cases, you might find that a partner who's putting a lot of time commitment into the deal isn't getting enough in return. This section will help avoid any issue down the road in case of disputes. It also helps clarify everyone's role in the project.

Asset Protection

How will the deal progress in case there's a lawsuit that affects one of you? This is where you will list the legal structure under which your deal will take place, and how each partner will be protected from risk. It also specifies how each partner will treat the assets of the legal structure, and how this will be marked as being different from their own personal assets.

Syndications

A syndicate is a term that is used to describe a group of investors who have pooled their money together in order to invest in real estate or any other asset. Technically speaking, the LPs that you set up will be a syndicate. Syndication allows you to raise capital from private investors and then deploy that capital in deals.

There is a lot of misinformation surrounding syndication, so it's worth taking the time to dispel these myths. The first myth is that you need to have worthy deals under your belt or under contract in order to convince people to invest with you.

This isn't true at all. It takes time to raise money and the last thing you want to be doing is raising it with a deadline staring you in the face. It takes time to build confidence and trust and therefore, you should seek investors well before you even begin sourcing deals. This way you'll have investors on hand when opportunity knocks.

There are a few securities laws you must follow when raising money for syndication. For starters, you cannot publicly advertise for capital. This means you cannot post ads online or on any other print media soliciting investments. If you do this, you'll need to register as a public entity with the Securities and Exchange Commission (SEC), and this is going to cost you a ton of money and will require you to be of a certain size (*Real Estate Syndication*, 2020).

You can raise money from friends and family and from other people you come into contact with. You will need to have legally vetted operating agreements and other contracts in place to ensure all your investors' capital is safe, and that they have recourse in case the deal doesn't pan out.

Syndication might also require you to seek investment only from people who are considered accredited investors. These people have a net worth of one million dollars or more when their primary residence's value is removed from the equation. This depends on the amount of money you're trying to raise.

Generally speaking, despite the legal issues that surround syndication, raising money through this method isn't as daunting as it's often made out to be. Yes, you will need to work hard at rising capital but this is something you'll have to do anyway. Hire the services of a good attorney, and you'll be well-placed to raise the money you need.

Operating Agreements

Partnerships and LLCs are required to run according to their operating agreements. Let's take a look at the most important aspects of these legal documents and understand what they mean.

Capital Calls

If the project needs more money, how will this be raised and what will be the terms of contribution? How will the existing shareholders' interests be treated? All of this is outlined in this section. Make sure you have an experienced attorney draft this section for you, and discuss these terms with your investor in detail.

New Members

What terms will new members be offered upon entry into the partnership? Existing members might not want their ownership diluted, or even want new members to share some of the benefits that they receive. After all, they're the ones that absorbed the early stage risk. This point clarifies the conditions under which new members can be brought on board and the threshold of approval the manager needs in order to do this.

Distributions

Real estate deals typically pay their members a certain rate of interest every month, and then pay the majority of capital gains once the property is sold at the end of the deal's term. This section deals with how much these distributions will be and it's something that all investors must agree upon.

Keep in mind that the manager of the partnership might need the money to reinvest into the property. This makes fixing the percent of distributions at a manageable rate important.

Manager Replacement

If the members of the LLC or LP are unhappy with the manager, what is the process that they'll use to remove them? How many votes will be needed to remove the manager? The legal process will be outlined here.

Transferability

This section outlines the conditions under which the shares of the LLC or syndicate will be offered to new investors. Generally, the existing investors will have the right of first refusal. This means they'll be offered the new investment first, and only upon their rejection will new members be offered these securities.

Reporting and Taxes

When will the company report its financial statements, and when will taxes be paid? Companies can affix a date as the end of their financial year. This section will outline this information in detail.

Chapter 6:

Exit Strategies

Every great deal needs a great exit. It is the exit that helps investors in the deal realize the majority of profits. Without a predefined plan in place, you'll find that even the best of deals will likely go sour.

There are many different exit strategies you can use for your deals. Instead of copying and pasting a predefined exit strategy, it's far better to develop one for yourself.

Developing a Plan

There are a few tips you can adhere to in order to develop an exit plan that makes the most sense to you. Here they are in no particular order.

Criteria

How will you judge whether the investment has been a success or failure? Every investor must have predefined thresholds in place that allow them to quickly determine whether they need to exit or not. Keep in mind, that an exit might also involve cutting your losses short.

This is why I had mentioned that planning for the worst-case scenario is a good idea. It'll help you prepare for exit scenarios in case your investment doesn't quite go as planned. Set a monetary limit for your downside as well as your upside. While you want your upside to be as high as possible on the trade, it helps to affix a minimum profit that you're seeking from the deal.

This will help you identify how far you have to go to your exit, and will greatly simplify the decision of whether to exit or not.

Goals

Closely tied to fixing your exit criteria are your investment goals. What are your short-term and long-term goals and how will the deal help you get there? If you hit some of these goals, perhaps it's time to consider an exit.

Market Conditions

Sometimes, deals can be exited on the basis of certain market conditions. Interest rates might make financing a poor deal for you. In such conditions, it might be better to take an early exit rather than hold on and try to eke out those final few points of profit from the deal.

Time

Exit goals can also be tied to time. If you wish to hold on to the property for not more than a year, thanks to hard money financing, then this provides you with a clear exit strategy. Take a look at the practical aspects of your deal and evaluate whether a time-based exit makes sense.

Sometimes, financing will make it such that you'll have to exit within a specific time. If you have a four year interest-only loan in place, that is tied to a property development deal, then this will be your exit timeline too.

Liquidity

Liquidity is all important when it comes to real estate deals. This is simply a measure of how much cash you have on hand to finance the project. If you find yourself running out of cash, consider an exit instead of raising even more money. This depends on the deal, but an early exit, due to a lack of liquidity, might provide you and your investors with better returns than prolonging your time spent in the deal.

While these tips will help you figure out what your exit strategy needs to be, here are some of the most common mistakes to avoid.

Mistakes to Avoid

The biggest mistake of all to avoid, is to not have a plan in place. As I said previously, every good real estate deal needs an exit. If you don't have one in place, then how exactly are you planning on making money on the deal? It doesn't make any business sense. Considering different exit strategies will help you place yourself in prime position to evaluate your different options.

Real estate offers many different exit strategies, so planning your exit will help you figure out which one suits you the best.

Not Keeping Tabs on Portfolio Worth

You must always know what your portfolio or deal is worth before you exit. This goes without saying, but many investors get caught up in collecting cash that they fail to recognize the capital gains rise in their portfolios. This means they fail to capitalize on what the market is offering them.

While you don't need to check what the property value is every single day, staying up to date with regard to developments in the market and what your properties are worth is always a good idea. Besides, it'll help you decide on a sale price that is on par with market prices.

Not Being Proactive

You will have to anticipate and read the signs in order to successfully exit your deals. The market might change overnight, and while you cannot foresee every single disaster on the horizon, you will have to do your best to avoid the ones you're capable of avoiding. Be proactive with regard to risk, and don't be forced to exit because of bad circumstances.

Quick Exits

Sometimes investors simply want to get rid of properties, but it pays to hold on to them for the most part. Quick exits usually mean the properties are not being valued properly, and that the investors are reacting to their circumstances instead of calmly assessing the situation. There are exceptions, of course, but it's hard to think of times when a quick exit is always a good idea.

Accepting the First Offer

There's an unwritten rule in real estate that whenever the first price or offer is accepted, both parties are left unhappy. The seller feels they gave in too soon, and the buyer feels they could have gotten a better price for the deal. When looking to exit a deal, don't blindly say yes to the first offer you get, no matter how desperately you wish to exit.

Take your time with it and negotiate a better price. Always.

Conclusion

You've done all the work and have crafted the best exit strategy. You've moved all your pieces perfectly, but then the unexpected happens and now you're left with a scenario on your hands that you hadn't planned for. How do you exit such deals?

The unexpected often happens in business, and thankfully, real estate offers a wide variety of exit strategies for the investor. Here are some of them:

1. Buy and hold - You could simply keep hanging onto your investment and refinance it in order to take advantage of better interest rates. Even if you didn't qualify for traditional lending, properties under existing ownership usually do. The downside is your exit strategy is still unclear and will now be time or market based.

2. Offering financing - If the buyer cannot afford to make payments or arrange financing, sell the property by providing financing yourself. This gives you full control over the terms of the deal, and you'll earn money via interest. The

downside is that you'll have to deal with defaults by yourself.

3. Prehab - If you've run out of cash before your property has been fully rehabbed, you can sell the property to another rehabber as a prehabbed property. This refers to when an investor spruces up the property to a certain extent thereby making the task easier for a flipper. The downside is that you won't make too much money on such deals unless the property was really run down.

4. Wholesaling - you could simply sell the property as is, even if you haven't completed any work on it. Wholesaling homes is a great way to get started in real estate and is an investment strategy by itself. However, it can be tough to pull off, and experienced investors use it to get themselves out of a jam if cash runs out.

5. Flipping - We've looked at this already. If you need to exit an investment, you can simply sell it outright or flip the property. This is a pretty conventional exit from an investment.

Real estate offers the ambitious entrepreneur a number of ways to make money. Even when you think there is no hope on the horizon, some exit strategy exists that will end up making you and your investors whole again. While this doesn't mean real estate is a sure-shot way of making money, you can rest assured that it is a tried and tested method of increasing your wealth.

As you've learned throughout this book, raising money for real estate isn't as daunting as it seems. A lot of work is required, but with the right level of dedication, you can raise all the money you need.

I wish you the best of luck with your capital raising efforts and hope to hear from you with regard to how this book has helped you!

Happy investing!

References

Capital raised for real estate investment pre-Covid-19 hits record high. (2020, April 15). www.propertyfundsworld.com. https://www.propertyfundsworld.com/2020/04/15/284716/capital-raised-real-estate-investment-pre-covid-19-hits-record-high

Choice of Entity Considerations for Real Estate Investors | EXETER 1031 Exchange Services, LLC |. (2020). www.exeter1031.com. http://www.exeter1031.com/choice_of_entity_considerations.aspx

Florentine, S., & Kapko, M. (2019, April 23). Why LinkedIn Premium is worth the money. CIO. https://www.cio.com/article/2877153/why-linkedin-premium-is-worth-the-money.html

Grozdanic, L. (2017, October 19). Top 5 Real Estate Accelerators Rethinking Urban Living. Archipreneur. https://archipreneur.com/top-5-real-estate-accelerators-rethinking-urban-living

Han, A. (2020). How to Pitch to Investors So They Bite. Www.Biggerpockets.Com. https://www.biggerpockets.com/blog/2013-08-12-how-to-pitch-to-investors

Hard Money 101: Everything You Need To Know About Getting Started With Hard Money Loans. (2015, April 6). REtipster. https://retipster.com/hard-money-101-everything-need-know-getting-started-hard-money-loans/

Merrill, T. (2020a, February 13). Understanding A Real Estate Partnership Agreement. FortuneBuilders. https://www.fortunebuilders.com/the-key-elements-of-a-real-estate-business-partnership-agreement/

Merrill, T. (2020b, May 18). Top 11 Real Estate Development Loans. FortuneBuilders. https://www.fortunebuilders.com/11-sources-to-finance-a-real-estate-business/

Real Estate Project Finance - Know Different Funding Types. (2020). Corporate Finance Institute. https://corporatefinanceinstitute.com/resources/knowledge/finance/real-estate-project-finance/

Real Estate Syndication | A Modern Guide to Real Estate Crowdfunding. (2020). CrowdStreet. https://www.crowdstreet.com/real-estate-syndication/

Top Questions Angel Investors Will Ask Entrepreneurs. (2016, July 12). Rockies Venture Club. https://www.rockiesventureclub.org/uncategor

ized/top-questions-angel-investors-will-ask-entrepreneurs/